HURT VILLAGE

BY KATORI HALL

★

★

DRAMATISTS
PLAY SERVICE
INC.

NOTE ON BILLING
Anyone receiving permission to produce HURT VILLAGE is required to give credit to the Author as sole and exclusive Author of the Play on the title page of all programs distributed in connection with performances of the Play and in all instances in which the title of the Play appears, including printed or digital materials for advertising, publicizing or otherwise exploiting the Play and/or a production thereof. The name of the Author must appear on a separate line, in which no other name appears, immediately beneath the title and in size of type equal to 50% of the size of the largest, most prominent letter used for the title of the Play. No person, firm or entity may receive credit larger or more prominent than the Author. The following acknowledgment must appear on the title page in all programs distributed in connection with performances of the Play:

World Premiere originally produced by
Signature Theatre Company, New York City
James Houghton, Founding Artistic Director
Erika Mallin, Executive Director

SPECIAL NOTE ON SONGS/RECORDINGS
Dramatists Play Service neither holds the rights to nor grants permission to use any songs or recordings mentioned in the Play. Permission for performances of copyrighted songs, arrangements or recordings mentioned in this Play is not included in our license agreement. The permission of the copyright owner(s) must be obtained for any such use. For any songs and/or recordings mentioned in the Play, other songs, arrangements, or recordings may be substituted provided permission from the copyright owner(s) of such songs, arrangements or recordings is obtained; or songs, arrangements or recordings in the public domain may be substituted.

HURT VILLAGE received its world premiere at the Signature Theatre Company (James Houghton, Founding Artistic Director; Erika Mallin, Executive Director) in New York City on February 27, 2012. It was directed by Patricia McGregor; the set and projection designs were by David Gallo; the costume design was by Clint Ramos; the lighting design was by Sarah Sidman; the sound design was by Robert Kaplowitz; the wig and makeup designs were by Cookie Jordan; the original music was by Luqman Brown; the fight director was Rick Sordelet; and the choreography was by Daniel Price. The cast was as follows:

COOKIE . . . . Joaquina Kalukango
CRANK . . . . Marsha Stephanie Blake
BIG MAMA . . . . Tonya Pinkins
BUGGY . . . . Corey Hawkins
TOYIA . . . . Saycon Sengbloh
CORNBREAD . . . . Nicholas Christopher
EBONY . . . . Charlie Hudson, III
SKILLET . . . . Lloyd Watts
TONY C . . . . Ron Cephas Jones

3

CHARACTERS
(in order of appearance)

COOKIE — (13 years old) Crank and Buggy's daughter, precocious and gifted, a wannabe rapper, just wants to get out.

CRANK — (late 20s) three years clean off of crack, hustles the government and does everybody hair in the neighborhood, cranky, has been taken in by Big Mama, used to date Buggy.

BIG MAMA — (55 years old) the matriarch of the family and respected hard-working pillar of the community, Buggy's blood grandmother.

BUGGY — (late 20s) a soldier returning home from the Iraq War with a haunting secret.

TOYIA — (late 20s) the fast-talking, loud-mouthed upstairs neighbor, works as an exotic dancer at the local "shake junt," Cornbread's "babymama," calls herself a feminist.

CORNBREAD — (late 20s) mixed-race or "high yella," FedEx employee and small-time drug dealer (also called "doughboy"), not-so-secretly in love with Crank.

EBONY — (late teens) neighborhood comedian and small-time doughboy, a Tony C crony.

SKILLET — (early to mid-teens) badly scarred from a childhood accident involving a skillet, speaks really slowly.

TONY C — (early 40s) The "Kang" of the doughboys and controls the crack houses in Hurt Village.

PLACE

Hurt Village. Memphis, Tennessee.

TIME

The end of summer. Second Bush Dynasty.

HURT VILLAGE

ACT ONE

Prologue

"The Past is Prologue"

Dusk. Somewhere the sky is falling into the ground. Bits and pieces of magenta, peach, and coral hues make the broken bits of beer bottles and crack vials glow with a stardust twinkle. No grass. No one. Dust rolls across this beautiful broken land like wisps of cotton candy blowing in the country wind. Except cotton candy does not exist in this modern-day waste-land. Nothing even remotely related to sweetness exists here. A crooked, dinted, weather-beaten sign that says "Hurt Village" sways in the wind. A two-tiered housing project served up Southern-style. Shattered windows. A constellation of garbage and debris. Broken-down burned-out cars. Dingy, tattered shirts and socks hang on for dear life to sagging clotheslines. The ghosts of hopscotch marks fade into the ground. A fading graffiti tag that says, "Das Haus des jammers" is splashed across one of the crumbling walls of the project. It looks as if a wrecking ball has already slammed through the sides, expos-ing the units. The faint outline of the Memphis Arena Pyramid glistens into existence in the distance. In the emerg-ing darkness, a chorus of children sweetly sings:

CHILDREN.
Hurt Village is falling down, falling down, falling down
Hurt Village is falling down, my fair bitches
Hurt Village is falling down, falling down, falling down
Hurt Village is falling down, my fair bitches.

5

(Lights up on Cookie, a thirteen-year-old flat-chested woman-child with a colorful array of barrettes hanging onto her greasy plaits. She is beating on the army green electric utility box in the front yard area with her small fists. She provides a steady bass accented by a quick rat-tat-tat at the end. As she flows, the sky drops further into the land, until — one by one — the unit lights of the housing project flicker on to light the night.)
COOKIE.
This be the war/ungh/this be the war/ungh
This be the war/ungh/this be the war/ungh, ungh
This be the war/ungh/this be the war/ungh
Ungh/

You can't see the stars no more/
Just the bling from the dreams of souls searching for the
    same thing/
For a lift of light from cavin' ceilings/
This my ode to project people strugglin'/
Mamas and fathers hold yo' daughters/
I'm precocious/most here know this and they know I spit the
    illest shit/
I spin ghetto tales that'll make you weep/
My lyrical lullabyes'll knock yo' ass to sleep/

'Cause I be the street storyteller/
Runnin' crackers through my hellah/
Ringin' the bells and yellin' through the wire like Mariah/
Having CNN on fire/

Bye bye to crumblin' walls/
Bye Bye to Auction Street/
Bye Bye too many sold/
Bye Bye too many beat

They makin' niggahs extinct/
too many drugs in the jail meat/
Chickenheads ain't comin' home to roost/
And Welfare man stopped sellin' Juicy Juice/

Ain't gone have nobody to play with afterwhile/
… while … while

Shit! I done got off my rhyme. *(Cookie looks out into the audience.)* Remember when the candylady used to live on the Seventh Street side of the complex? You could get them pink chewys for two cents a dollop. You can't buy shit for two cents no mo'. E'erthang cost nearbout a dollar. Inflation. Fuck Bush! Remember when we use to play curbball? Object of the game: you had to stand on yo' porch and hit the curb of yo' neighbors porch with a ball. If you hit they curb, you got a point. If it bounced back and hit yours, you got a double. Hell, yeah! I was the queen of muthafuckin' curbball. Wun't nobody betta than me. Or how 'bout when folks'll be outside playin' "Hide the Belt"? You'd take yo' mama's most favoritist belt she whip you wit' and somebody like, Ray-Ray or Peaches, would go behind the complex and hide it. When they fount it, e'erbody would break for the base 'cause whoever got the belt could beat the shit out of e'erbody! Base'll be somebody porch that had a couch on it so you could sit down and catch yo' breath after runnin' so hard. I still got welts 'til this day. I couldn't run for shit. Us project kids cleverah than a muthafucka, maine. Mmph, mmph, mmph them was the days. 'Fo' it got bad. I mean Hurt Village always been bad, but it done got *bad-bad*, like you-betta-move-yo-Big-Mama-out-these-muthafuckin-projects-'fo'-she-get-gang-raped-robbed-and-murdered-by-her-Gangsta Disciple crack head son bad. Yeah, we done seen some thangs livin' on the Old Thomas side. Folks from all over Memphis know our street as the Million Dollar Track. You can get yo' crack, smack, dro, *and* you can catch a bullet. Children can't even go outside to play no mo'. I ain't played Curbball in I don't know how long. They done already moved a lota folk out. We the last ones. That why Big Mama been bein' cheap. She been savin' up her scrilla for a minute for when we move to our new house. Oooooo, Big Mama know she been bein' cheap as HELL. Memphis be hot as a muthafucka in the summer and she don't be lettin' a niggah turn on the air conditioner for mo' than fifteen minutes at a time. Always yakkin', "You gone run up the light bill." She'en even have to pay for 'lectricity! They give that shit to us for free! But I guess po' folk always gotsta be savin' they scrilla. Like take Dawn dishwashin' liquid for instance. That stuff's the shit, ain't it? It's for more than just dishes. It body wash, washin' detergent, Windex, bubble bath, Barbie shampoo … Yeah, maine. Folks round here so po' we can't even afford the r at the end. Project niggahs have to think fast, cry later. Livin' o'er here can try you sometimes. I done had fun though. But I'm thirteen, and I'm a grown ass woman now. *(Crank, Cookie's mother, enters, striking a clenched-fist-on-hip pose on the cracked concrete porch.)*

CRANK. Cookie! Get yo' ass up in here. You know you suppose-ta be in this house befo' them skreet lights come on. When them lightnin' bugs start lightin' they asses, yo' ass need to be lightnin' up in here. I'n gone tell you no more, nah!

COOKIE. *(Indicating the broken street light.)* The skreet light broke. How I'm supposeta know when it time to come in?

CRANK. You know you got yo' first day of school in the mornin.'

COOKIE. So!

CRANK. Cookie! Don't make me come out there and yank you! And keep on sittin' on that 'lectricity box. Yo' booty gone blow up.

COOKIE. Yes, ma'am! *(To the audience.)* Maine, I can't wait to move on up out of here.

Scene 1

"Bombs Over Baghdad"

Inside the unit. Cardboard boxes are scattered everywhere. They are packing. It is sparsely furnished with that black lacquered rent-to-own furniture made out of more sawdust than actual wood. The TV is on its last leg, hence the aluminum foil to give a signal. Music videos are on — as usual. There are cracks in the cement walls, which are painted a deep peeling burgundy. There is the drone of crunk music blaring from car speakers outside, perhaps classic Three 6 Mafia.* You can hear an occasional bottle thrown to the ground accented by yells from the guys outside.

COOKIE. I don't wanna get my hair did!

CRANK. I'dn know why you whinin' for.

COOKIE. I wanna go outside and play!

CRANK. No child of mine gone be runnin' round like a cat been

* See Special Note on Songs and Recordings on copyright page.

suckin' on her head.

COOKIE. Ma!

CRANK. You hear 'bout that lil' girl on Seventh Skreet?

COOKIE. Naw …

CRANK. Had a little girl over there didn't like to get her hair did. Jus' wouldn't let her mama comb her head. Braids was just a hangin' on by a strand. So her mama left her braids in for two years. One day, da girl come to school and say her head hurtin.' Nobody believe her. Next week she was dead. Come to find out a spider came in the middle of the night, set up a nest in her head and sucked all the blood out.

COOKIE. That's a urban legend!

CRANK. That ain't no legend. Bet!

COOKIE. You just a lie — (Crank smacks Cookie on the head with the comb. Enter Big Mama, the matriarch, who rules her house with a sharp tongue and an iron fist.)

BIG MAMA. Don't be callin' yo' mama a lie, even though she can't tell the truth worth shit. I should pull one of her gold teeth out e'ertime she lie. Call her "a story."

COOKIE. You a story!

BIG MAMA. Just look at that chile head. Look like a cat been suckin' on it.

CRANK. I tolt her! If she would just sit down, her head would done been combed by nah. Next time, I'ma let you go to school nappy-headed.

BIG MAMA. Girl, I'll stomp a cone in yo' ass you let that girl go to school lookin' like that.

CRANK. Ugggh! I'm so glad y'all goin' back. So I can go on my vacation.

COOKIE. Ma, seem like you always on vacation. Whatchoo gone do when I'm at school?

BIG MAMA. Sit on her narrow behind and collect a check. That's what she gone do. I done been on my feet all damn night. I ain't gone work that night shift no more. Folks down at the VA 'bout to run me ragged.

CRANK. If you didn't work so much, yo' check'll be more.

BIG MAMA. Honey, that Welfare ain't 'bout shit. And I'm too young for some Social Security. I gotta work. What I need to do is collect me a muthafuckin' crazy check. 'Cause y'all about to run me crazy. Speakin' a crazy. You crazy you thank you gone lay up here all day

9

watchin' TV and not work. *You* need to call yoself findin' you a job.

CRANK. *(Irritably.)* I'm finna go to cosmetology school —

BIG MAMA. "Finna go" don't put no food on the table. Shit! I don't know why somebody wanna waste money on cosmetology school when everything you need to know you can learn in that kitchen.

CRANK. If I'ma have my own shop, I'ma need a license to practice.

BIG MAMA. What you need a license for? You might work on folk heads, but you ain't no muthafuckin' brain surgeon. You still needs to get yoself a job.

CRANK. I make 'nuf money fixin' folks hair. I gets my cash under the table, then my Welfare check, *and* a crazy check. I'm rollin'. All — what them folks be sayin' — tax exempt." Besides, Oprah say —

BIG MAMA. Don't pull that Oprah-follow-yo'-dreams-bullshit on me. I had a dream once. I had a dream that by the time I was fifty-five I'd have my house to myself and wouldn't have to feed and raise no more chillen. I done already had mine, and I'm still raisin' chillen. And Crank, you ain't even none of mine. I took you in 'cause you had a baby by my grandson, but as long as you live under my roof, you gone do as I say. I might not a brought you in this world, but I sho as hell —

ALL. "can take you OUT of it."

BIG MAMA. I sho'll will. Nah, how come y'all ain't rippin' through these boxes? Y'all know them housing folk comin' to move us by next Friday.

CRANK. "Movin on up! To Raleigh! We finally got a piece of the piieeeeeeee!"

BIG MAMA. Is you *back* on crack?

CRANK. No.

BIG MAMA. Betta not be. You get on that shit again, I'll really stomp a cone in yo' ass. *(Cookie looks out the lone window.)*

COOKIE. Where all these niggahs gone go?

BIG MAMA. Honey, the hell if I know. The city suppose to move us everywhichaway but the right way. But they movin' *us* the right way. We movin' out to Raleigh, the best 'burb in M-town.

CRANK. Niggahs just gone move over to the white folks' neighborhood and fuck they shit up.

BIG MAMA. Well, white folks can keep on movin' out east 'til they nearbout fall in the ocean. Fuck 'em. Ouch! *(Cookie has dropped a big-ass box on Big Mama's foot.)* What the hell wrong with you droppin' that big-ass box on my gotdang toe! Y'all know folks with sugar feets be hurtin' and some more shit. *(She takes off her shoe to inspect her feet. Sucks her teeth.)* Need to get my damn foot shaved. Cookie, hand me a beer out the 'frigerator. *(Cookie goes and gets the beer for Big Mama.)*

COOKIE. It's hot.

BIG MAMA. That 'frigerator just stay broke. *(Cookie kicks the refrigerator it. It turns back on again.)* Where my mail at? My JC Penney catalog come?

CRANK. Cookie was sittin' on it.

BIG MAMA. Well, I hope you done washed yo' booty. Betta not be no crabs crawlin' on it. *(Crank covers Cookie's ears.)*

COOKIE. What she talkin' 'bout?

CRANK. Nothin'

BIG MAMA. I am talkin' 'bout somethin'! S-T-D —

CRANK. Shhhhheee don't need to know 'bout all that!

BIG MAMA. How come she don't? Hell, you had her when you was thirteen —

CRANK. Ain't it time fo' you to go to bed so you'll be ready fo' yo' shift tonight?

BIG MAMA. Not befo' I make my list. When they move us out to Raleigh, this what I'ma have in my house. Y'all need to learn how to make ya goals. Write that shit down on paper. When it wrote ain't no denyin' it. *(She gazes at the catalog.)* Ohhhh, look at that recliner ... Gone look good in my new livin' room. We is gone have a livin' room *and* a dinin' room, ye'en know? Oooooo! I got my Publishers Clearin' House! *(She fans that yellow envelope in the air.)*

CRANK. There she go ...

BIG MAMA. We gone win our million dollars if I keep on sendin' these jokers in!

CRANK. You and yo' bougie dreams.

BIG MAMA. Hell, one day I'ma win! And y'all ain't gone get na'an one penny! I'ma get me a house out by the white folk by my damn self. Cookie, go get me my pocketbook for me a stamp.

COOKIE. You'd think that'd let you mail it in for free they got millions of dollars. *(Cookie goes to get Big Mama's pocketbook on the counter. Crank continues to shift through the boxes.)*

CRANK. These junts is heavy.

COOKIE. Books?

CRANK. How it's gone be some books?

COOKIE. I don't know. You said it was heavy. I *ascertained* it might be some books.

CRANK. You ass-a-wha?

COOKIE. Assumed. Divined. Hypothesized — *(Crank pops Cookie upside the head.)*

CRANK. Come over here and help me move it! / Tryin' to be all smart and shit.

BIG MAMA. Crank, don't you hit that chile in my presence. *(Beat. Crank looks at Cookie who holds her head in pain.)*

CRANK. Fine. Go clean up that room 'fore you go to school. Look like a damn tornado done ripped through it.

COOKIE. Maaaaaaaaaaaaiiiiiiiiiiiiinnnnnnnnnnnneeeeeeeeee! *(Cookie stomps off.)*

CRANK. I don't wanna hear no nothin' comin' out yo' mouth! I'm tired of you back talkin', nah. *(Beat.)* She just done got to bein' hard-headed. Don't wanna mind nobody.

BIG MAMA. She just don't wanna mind *you.* That's what y'all get for havin' 'em so young. Hell, Cookie might as well be yo' lil' sistah. *(There is a knock on the screen door.)*

CRANK. Who dat is?

BIG MAMA. Clearly, the Prize Patrol or somebody that wanna get shot. *(Big Mama goes to the screen door, but she stops dead in her tracks. Big Mama's eyes change. The harsh glaze her eyes hid behind has dropped; curtain down. We see this strong woman cave into herself — sag like the branches of a weeping willow — but just for a moment. Buggy, her long lost grandson, opens the screen door and walks inside the unit. He wears a wife beater sticky with sweat. His muscles squished like sausages into a shirt that can barely contain his chest. He is a man. He lifts his marine jacket off his shoulder. His pants are cuffed into sandy black boots that have been attacked by ghetto dust balls. The one that got out. Gorgeous, he is: deep bronze skin with the slanted eyes of an Angolan warrior. He stands there.)* Lawd, have mercy on my soul. We done thought you was dead.

BUGGY. No, ma'am. They sent me home … rightfully so.

BIG MAMA. How come you ain't tole nobody? We coulda picked you up from the airport. Got Cornbread 'nem to pick you up.

BUGGY. I thought I'd save y'all the trouble. So I walked.

BIG MAMA. Boy, how you gone walk all the way from 'cross town in this heat? You gone have a stroke.

BUGGY. I done been to some hotter places, Big Mama. Heat ain't never kilt nobody.

BIG MAMA. How come it ain't? Them high school boys be fallin' out at football practice all the time playin' in that hot-ass sun —

BUGGY. Ain't nobody playin' football, Big Mama —

BIG MAMA. Come here and let me look at ya. *(Buggy hugs his grandmother.)* My grandson … Yo' mama woulda been so proud of you. Servin' yo' country, boy. Makin' niggahs over here proud. How come you ain't tell nobody you was comin'?

BUGGY. Didn't know I was comin' back 'til it happened.

BIG MAMA. Yeah, life'll do that to you. *(Beat.)*

BUGGY. Crank.

CRANK. I'm surprised you 'member me.

BUGGY. Always. *(Beat. Big Mama breaks the uncomfortable silence.)*

BIG MAMA. Damn, you done got swole. What they feedin' folk over there?

BUGGY. They sho'll don't feed nobody no pig feet, hog mogs, or collard greens.

BIG MAMA. Ooooooo, that what we gone have tonight!

CRANK. Big Mama, I done already packed up the *big* pots.

BIG MAMA. So! We gone have us a party. Tell everybody my lil' Buggy done come on home.

BUGGY. Awwww, Big Mama, don't call me that. That ain't befittin' a soldier.

BIG MAMA. I don't care what they call you over there, Artelius. Here you "Buggy!" Cookie, come on in here and see yo' daddy.

COOKIE. *(Offstage.)* I'm a freak of nature: I ain't got no daddy.

BUGGY. I know that ain't who I thank it is. *(Cookie runs in and stops at the door.)*

COOKIE. Who the hell he?

CRANK. You'un 'member him?

BUGGY. She done got stout. She wun't nothin' 'bout three when I seen't her last.

CRANK. That was right before …

BIG MAMA. Yo' mama passed.

BUGGY. Yeah.

CRANK. Yeap.

BUGGY. You look just like yo' mama.

BIG MAMA. Honey, two peas in a pod. Can't barely tell one from the other. They wear the same size shoe, too.

COOKIE. I hope you brought us somethin' from overseas like

13

other folks do. I heard you can get some fresh Air Force Ones on the low-low, you know though.

BUGGY. How old you now?

BIG MAMA. Honey, thirteen goin' on thirty.

BUGGY. Well, kids 'round here grow up fast.

BIG MAMA. Sho'll do. Unh, unh, unh. I need to get on yo' exercise program. Done left and went and got fine on ya grandmama. I'ma have to starve myself. They need to lock the 'frigerator up 'cause I done got to lookin' bigger than a barge!

COOKIE. Ain't nothin' up in there to eat no way. We woulda had had somethin' up in here, if Crank hadna popped off the food stamps.

BIG MAMA. Who you done popped off my food stamps to?

CRANK. Don't worry 'bout it. You gone get yours. I done got fifty dollars for a sixty-five-dollar book.

COOKIE. How you gone pop off a sixty-five-dollar book for fifty dollars? That don't make no sense.

CRANK. Cuz nobody wanna use them fucked-up-ass food stamps.

COOKIE. I suppose they less attractive, but check this. They savin' more 'cause a sixty-five-dollar book is really worth seventy dollars of groceries 'cause you ain't gotta pay tax on a book. They gettin' seventy dollars' worth of food for fifty dollars. That's just stupid business right there. That's why niggahs be broke right now. They don't know howta handle they business.

BUGGY. She smaaaart. Know how to make a dollar, huh?

COOKIE. I'm tryin' to save me up a little cash pot. I got a album comin' out.

CRANK. She be lockin' herself up in the bathroom. Rappin' into her little funky Fisher-Price tape recorder.

COOKIE. That all I got, maine.

BUGGY. So you a rapper? You gone flow for me?

COOKIE. I'll think about it.

BUGGY. Gone spit me a couple of bars. *(Cookie blushes.)*

CRANK. Don't be shame, nah! *(Buggy starts beating on the cement wall. Cookie finally gains some confidence.)*

COOKIE.
    Lil' bitches be rappin'
    Fingers poppin' on the corner
    Be poppin' they pussy
    But they don't really mean it though
    Niggahs tryta look at me

But can't step to me correctly
Niggah don't perpetrate
I'm just trying to percolate
Whut! Whut! whut! whut!
Straight up off the dome, son.
(She starts jookin' in circles.)
BIG MAMA. Why these young folks don't sing no more. Just be boppin' they gums.
COOKIE. I'm expressin' myself! Hell, it's war out on these skreets.
CRANK. You don't know what war is.
BUGGY. That was *awesome! (Uncomfortable silence.)*
COOKIE. Why you talk funny?
CRANK. 'Cause he a oreo. Always been one. You gone be one too in a little while 'cause you finna' be bussed over to them cracker schools. *(Cornbread, a mixed race or "high yella" old friend of Buggy's, knocks on the screen door. Then he comes in. Decked out in navy blue and orange, he sports FedEx proudly on his shirt. Toyia enters with him, his "babymama." They are so engrossed in their fight that they don't notice Buggy standing in the kitchen corner.)*
TOYIA. Girl, I need to borrow a cup of warshin' powder.
CRANK. For what?
TOYIA. I need to douche this niggah sperm out my muthafuckin' pussy. What you thank!
CORNBREAD. Ain't nobody done put they dick up in you.
CRANK. Don't be talkin' like that round my chile.
TOYIA. She gone find out soon enough. See, Cookie listen to me 'cause this here a cautionary tale. Don't let na'an one niggah trick you into havin' a baby that even they don't want cause, you see, they be the first ones to keep on steppin' down the line when you need some Pampers, some Similac, some shoes, or some bail. Always screamin' and hollerin' 'bout how, "It too expensive! It too expensive!" but when you axe him for four hundred dollars for a abortion, niggah don't wanna give it, but, that's yo' fault niggah. I told ya so! That's yo' fault niggah. That's yo' fault, so hell, yeah, you gone take care of me now. Don't pay up then, you pay ten times later. Wha! Wha!
CORNBREAD. Somebody please but a dick in her mouth.
TOYIA. I done already had one and it wun't yo's —
BIG MAMA. Ay! Ay! Ay! It's called a condom!
TOYIA. My bad, Big Mama. I didn't barely see you over there.
BIG MAMA. Well, get some muthafuckin' glasses then. *(Toyia*

finally notices Buggy.)

TOYIA. I'm sorry, ma'am. But bump some glasses. I needs me a muthafuckin' microscope. *(She sashays over to Buggy.)* Who this fine speci-man chillin' up in the cut?

CORNBREAD. Keep yo' project paws to yo'self. It ain't nobody for you. This my niggah. My niggah! Awwwwww, playa president, wha! Wha!!

BUGGY. Cornbread!

CORNBREAD. You been shipped outta here for more than a Memphis minute!

BUGGY. Yeah, but I'ma be back for a while.

TOYIA. You done come back for the high school reunion?

CORNBREAD. Toyia, you ain't even graduate.

TOYIA. Niggah, you ain't neither! *(Looking him up and down.)* You look real different from high school though. Don't he Crank?

CRANK. He look … betta. *(Beat. She busies herself, continuing to pack. Crank picks up Cookie's dollhouse.)*

COOKIE. Unh, unh! You can't throw that away.

CRANK. Why not? You don't play wit' it no more.

COOKIE. It's a testament to my childhood.

CORNBREAD. *(To Cookie.)* Don't mind her!

CRANK. Cracker be gone.

CORNBREAD. I ain't white, twitchy-ass girl! I don't know how many times I gotta tell y'all funky ass.

CRANK. You betta be nice, or I'ma tell Toyia where I seen't you last Saturday.

TOYIA. Where you seen't him?

CRANK. On Beale lookin' drunker than a skunk. Believe that, playa. *(Toyia smacks him upside the head.)*

TOYIA. Just tell me when you cheatin'! That's all I axe, that's all I axe!

CORNBREAD. Maine, you got a Kool on you?

BUGGY. Always, always. *(They begin to light up.)*

BIG MAMA. Unh, unh. Parliaments the only thang I let be smoked up in here. Take that menthol shit on somewhere. *(Buggy and Cornbread exit the unit to smoke.)*

CORNBREAD. I love me some pussy, but it's just too much up in there. *(Beep. Beep. Cookie runs out past them.)*

COOKIE. *(To Cornbread.)* I need some lunch money. *(Cornbread digs into his pocket and pulls out several bills. She takes them and*

begins to run off.)
CORNBREAD. Ay, girl. *(She comes back, kisses him on the cheek.*
Runs off again.) She gettin' so big.
BUGGY. Yeah …
CORNBREAD. So, fuck witcha boy for a minute. What you been
eatin'?
BUGGY. What *you* been eatin'?
CORNBREAD. I been eatin' real good since I got me a job on the
"plantation."
BUGGY. Awww, damn maine.
CORNBREAD. Yeah, FedEx 'bout to have me throwin' my
muthafuckin' back out. Liftin' they heavy-ass boxes. Makin' five
dollars and a quarter on the hour.
BUGGY. Might as well be bent over pickin' cotton.
CORNBREAD. That what I know. But they the only ones hirin'
niggahs wit' a charge so … you know? Damn, niggah. It sho'll is
good as hell to see you. Glad I got to see you fo' they move us all out.
BUGGY. Glad I came, too, hell. Y'all wun't gone tell nobody?
CORNBREAD. Hell, niggah, you the one that done stopped
writin' folk, tellin' folk where you was at. We just thought the good
ole boy was in Heaven.
BUGGY. *(Looking around.)* This some sad shit —
CORNBREAD. Ain't it? But I guess it's for the best. They, uh, gone
flip these units. Memphis done got this thang — the HOPE grant.
Thirty-five million to make these here units into "mix income" 'part-
ments they sayin'. Hurt Village gone be turnt to Uptown Condos!
BUGGY. How dat gone work?
CORNBREAD. I dunno. Bougie-ass niggahs don't like to stay
nexta poor-ass niggahs, and white trash don't like to stay nexta nig-
gahs, so how they gone brew that pot of stew, I don't know. If you
axe me, look like they tryin' to mix shit up that don't need mixin'.
Just ask my ma and pop. Hell, I coulda told 'em that little recipe
ain't gone work.
BUGGY. You always talkin' food.
CORNBREAD. Hell, I'm always hungry. Don't tell the missus,
but, uhm, I done saved up enough money off that hustlin' …
BUGGY. Still on that track.
CORNBREAD. But, see I'm 'bout to be out the game, bra. *This*
the week I quit.
BUGGY. Yeah, niggah, whatever.

17

CORNBREAD. I'm fo' real! Playa, I'm workin' me a legit now. Fuck this shit. What Whitney Houston say? "Crack is whack!" The game ain't nothin' like it useta be. It useta be 'bout makin' a coupla dollars. Now, niggahs wanna kill ya' over a porch. I been doin' this shit e'er since high school. I'm tired, niggah. I asked God to let me hustle 'til I made it and I done did it. Gone get me and homegirl a mansion out in Mississippi. As crazy as she is, maine. I swear fo' God, this my last week. Hell, tell ya what. You come in be my right-hand man. The faster I sell it the faster I'm gone. I'll give you fifty skraight off the prof. *(Beat.)*

BUGGY. Niggah, I'm the protector of the United States. How I'ma be lookin' like slangin' rock on the porch?

CORNBREAD. 'Scuse me then ole-Ninja Turtle-lookin' ass niggah. Well, tell me about the war, then. You kilt some folks? *(Beat.)*

BUGGY. Yeah …

CORNBREAD. You look like you done kilt twenty niggahs whitcho bare hands and shit. Look at you, maine. Ye'en like us, maine, you done did somethin' witcho life. Maine, make me 'bout to cry up in this bitch. I heard you been stationed all over the world. Germany, Philippines, hell, now, Iraq.

BUGGY. Yeah, my tour of duty over so …

CORNBREAD. You probably got so much action out there maine. Poppin' them Muslim maniacs in they head.

BUGGY. Naw, it wun' like that, really.

CORNBREAD. Maine, you went over there to free that country. That some brave-ass shit. And I bet you can get pussy easy with that uniform.

BUGGY. *(Reluctant to divulge.)* Well …

CORNBREAD. Don't tell me you been bumpin' some niggah booty?

BUGGY. Hell, naw!

CORNBREAD. Hell, niggah, well I ain't know! You ain't answering me skraight so I'm askin' ya is ya crooked.

BUGGY. *(Deepening his voice.)* Hell, naw!

CORNBREAD. Just makin' sho'! It done got to be a epidemic down here. Now, I don't mind if a girl do that shit. That's sexy as hell. I went to the shake junt one night and saw two freaky deaks lookin' for that chewin.' Hell, that's what I'm pursuin'. *Lesbianos bes my favorito thingos, ye'en know?* Toyia, know. We got some funny niggahs runnin' round out here, now. All out in the open. It's terrible.

BUGGY. Why you so concerned with it?

CORNBREAD. Hell, somebody gotta be! Somebody gotta make sho' folks livin' right, ya know what I'm sayin'? *(Cornbread looks Buggy up and down.)* A solja. Done made it out. So to celebrate yo' homecomin' we gone have to take the boys out to the shake junt. Take you on that Pure Passion trip, ya know what I'm sayin'? Get you some pussy and some new tennie shoes 'cause it's tooooo hot for some boots. *(Broad daylight. There are the sounds of gunshots in the distance. Buggy jumps. Cornbread smiles.)* Welcome home, niggah.

Scene 2

"The Ring Shout"

The snapping ring. Ebony and Skillet are in their respective corners on the concrete, ready to duke it out. Buggy is watching his welcome-home festivities, leaned against someone's car, eating off a Styrofoam plate. Crank is on the porch eating popcorn. Toyia is on the upper level keeping score with her "ohhs and ahhs." In one corner, there is Skillet — a skinny tall, lanky boy with slurry speech, gold teeth, and a pick in his afro. He is badly burned on his face and legs, but he wears his scars proudly: his ghetto badge of honor. He is always putting cocoa butter on his burns. He speaks very slowly, so he can barely get a word out edge-wise.

In the other is, Ebony, the king of the checkers. He's the absolute don of the checking ring. He'd make Jesus cry. He has a greasy wave nouveau (Jheri curl wave at the top with shaved sides), gold teeth, shorts so long they could be his pants, a wifebeater, tattoos, and K-Swiss so white a helicopter could spot him from the sky. His rapid-fire rollin' delivery keeps the crowd entertained. Cornbread is barbecuing on a poor man's grill — a hinged oil barrel. And, as usual, he is instigating. Cookie is jookin' (a kind of Michael Jackson-esque urban ballet.) in the dirt. Everyone watches the game.

CORNBREAD. We have in one corner, Skillet otherwise known as the Coca-Butter Man.

ALL. Ooooohhhhhhh!

CORNBREAD. And in the other we have, the king of the checkers, Ebony. Let's get ready to ruuuuuummmmmble!

EBONY. Bumpy gum lookin'-ass, old broke ass mo'fo niggah.

SKILLET. Yo' mama so fat ... when she wear a Malcolm X jacket ... helicopters wanna land on her.

ALL. Booooooh!

CORNBREAD. You gone let him talk to you like that?

EBONY. Is that all you can come up with? Niggah, that cocoa butter ain't gone help you, it's gone make you crispier than you already is, you Krispy Kreme-ass crunchy black-ass niggah. Check this out y'all. Skillet house so stanky dat that when you go up in, it smell like the *Twilight Zone,* "Doo, doo, doo, doo. Doo, doo, doo, doo."

ALL. Oooohhh!

CORNBREAD. Where is yo balls, Skillet! Where is they?

SKILLET. Niggah ... fuck ... you ... and yo' ... mama!

EBONY. I can't, my mama died when she looked at yo' face.

ALL. Ooooooh!

CORNBREAD. It's gettin' crunk up in the Hurt.

TOYIA. Whut! Whut!

EBONY. You soooo broke, that when niggahs break into yo' house, they *leave* you money.

ALL. Ooooohhhhh!

EBONY. Wearin' them broke-down fake-ass Adidas them Mexican niggahs be wearin.' Fajitas.

ALL. Oooohhhhh! *(Toyia pipes in with a small baby balanced on her hip.)*

TOYIA. You leave him alone. I don't know why you always be pickin' on Skillet. You know he slow.

EBONY. Shut up witcho WIC Weetabix-weave-wearin' ass.

TOYIA. Yo' mama!

EBONY. *Yo'* mama, bitch ...

TOYIA. You just mad 'cause you can't get none of this, witcho greasy-hair ass. Can fry a bucket a chicken all that canola in yo' hair.

EBONY. Bitch, don't nobody want you. You so ugly, when niggahs come to the shake junt they don't give you dollars, they put pennies in yo panties.

TOYIA. Midnight-blue lookin' niggah, *fuck you.*

EBONY. *(To Cornbread.)* You can't turn a hoe into a housewife.

CORNBREAD. Ay, Ay, Ay —

TOYIA. And you can't make yo' lil'-ass dick longer than yo' belly button.

ALL. Oooooohhh!

SKILLET. Niggah ... You so black ... You ... piss ... coffee.

CORNBREAD. Nigggggah, boooooo!

EBONY. Naw, niggah least my blackness is natural. Yo' mama so stupid she thought leavin' a skillet of grease on the stove would warm up the house, but she burnt you up instead. Stupid ass bitch.

ALL. *(Low rumble.)* Oooooo.

CORNBREAD. It's gettin' personal up in the Hurt ...

TOYIA. Unh, unh. That just ain't right.

SKILLET.
I might be slow wit' my spit
But I'm quick to hit a bitch
Like yo' hoe sistah Peach
She ain't nothin' but a snitch
Yo' sistah is a lesbo
I fucked her real good
And so did everybody
In the whole damn hood.

(He literally pats himself on the back, gives himself a pound. He has never released something so quickly before. Someone provides a beat for Ebony. Ebony runs around the circle beefin' himself up.)

EBONY. Louder y'all! Turn it up! Check this out! *(Rat-tat-tat-tat-tat-tat.)*
Niggah, niggah on the wall who the fairest of them all
It ain't you, 'cause it's me, Kang of checkin', Ebony
I'ma tear you to the roodoo tooda. I'm gone wreck this place
'Cause you in my crunk-ass circle, muthafucka

ALL.
Kill yo'self fool!
Kill yo'self fool!

EBONY. In my circle, I swear fo' God you'll be stomped fool!

ALL.
Kill yo'self fool!
Kill yo'self fool!

EBONY. You steppin' up too close to the checkin' King fool!

> These words are like tornados, my breath like earthquakes
> I see yo' chest pumpin' hard, yo' knees beginnin' ta shake
> Babies are scared of you. Niggah, I'm scared of you
> It ain't nothin' new about it, you'se a ugly-ass dude
>
> You so ugly look like the Devil done shit upon yo' face
> You ain't never gone get pussy, betta start yo' paper chase
> 'Cause you can't ever step up to me wit' whack-ass rhymes
> That don't cost a goddamn dollar, a quarter or a dime
>
> This is skraight off the dome, this spit-fire crunk-ass poem
> Don't step up to me, I'll run yo' monkey-ass home
> Fry you like a piece of bologna and pop you in the middle
> Then burn you up again and flip you in my fuckin' *skillet.*

CORNBREAD. Whut! Whut! WHUT! WHUT! WHUT! WHUT!
(Ebony has won the verbal match, as usual. The women dance and make ululuation-esque sounds. They all start gangsta walking. And they break out into their well-known chant, the "Hurt Village Anthem." They pick up various props: a metal barrel, a pole, empty glass bottles from the trash surrounding the complex. This garbage becomes ad-hoc instruments in their own make-shift orchestra pit.)
ALL.

> We gone keep it real crunk
> Keep it, keep it real loud
> Bump all you bitches
> Bump, bump all these fake HOES
> We know how to keep it real crunk
> Keep it real loud
> Fuck all you niggahs who don't know what we talkin' 'bout.
>
> We gone keep it real crunk
> Keep it, keep it real loud
> Bump all you bitches
> Bump, bump all these fake HOES
> We know how to keep it real crunk
> Keep it real loud
> Fuck all you niggahs who don't know what we talkin' 'bout.

CORNBREAD. Who run this!?!?

ALL. We do!
CORNBREAD. Who run this?
ALL. We run this!
CORNBREAD. Who run this?
ALL. We do!
CORNBREAD. Y'all scared?
ALL. I'n scared!
CORNBREAD. Y'all scared?
ALL. I'n scared!
CORNBREAD. Who gone get crunk in our muthafuckin' circle?
(Cookie jumps in.)
COOKIE.

    I'm sick 'n' tired a bein' sick 'n' tired
    A walkin' through the skreets
    Fellahs starin' or they glarin'
    Some grinnin' past gold teeth
    Now, they say they wanna take care of me
    'Cause I'm a victim of real bad case of TB

    Titties and booty, it's double duty, I'm thirteen
    The corner boys never stop talkin' rude and
    They either call me a bitch or hoe
    'Cause to they toe-up-ass car, this "bitch" won't go

    Y'all know the type that be in his brother's ride
    Like to lean to the back and then lean to the side
    Always be bumpin' the latest Triple Six
    "Bitch, come over here and suck my dick!"

    And dis here be the killin' part 'bout it
    Y'all just playin' hopscotch on the Hurt Village lot and
    This niggah come and fuck up ya concentration
    You ignore his fellatio verbal penetration

    But then he try to get out the car
    "Niggah, do you really wanna catch a rape charge?"
    "Fuck you then, you siddity-ass bitch."
    Got the nerve to get mad
    'Cause he the one done flipt the script

I don't care about the scrilla
Runnin' roun' in yo' pockets
Or that ya got a dingaling
That's as long as a rocket
Yo wee wee won't take me there
And yes, niggah this is my rullllllll hair

So there, keep runnin' yo' fake-ass game
Fo' I say somethin' that'll make you feel real shame
Whut! Whut! WHUT! WHUT! WHUT! WHUT!

ALL.
We gone keep it real crunk
Keep it, keep it real loud
Bump all you bitches
Bump, bump all these fake HOES
We know how to keep it real crunk
Keep it real loud
Fuck all you niggahs who don't know what we talkin' 'bout!!

(The Village gathers around Cookie, celebrating her.)

BUGGY. That's my girl!

CRANK. That's *my* girl!

EBONY. That shit don't count. Lil' bitches can't step up up in the ring! I couldn't half understand what she was sayin'!

TOYIA. Niggah, 'cause you ain't gotcho GED.

COOKIE. I used a dictionary *and* a thesaurus on yo' ass.

ALL. Check!

EBONY. That ain't fair!

CORNBREAD. Don't matter, niggah. Can't help it ye'en know what she was sayin'!

SKILLET. I could understand it shorley. You got punked by a little girl, muthafucka! *(Ebony rises to confront Skillet.)* What niggah! You ready to die today? *(Ebony puts a finger in his face.)*

EBONY. Ain't nobody gone do nathan but penetration to yo' ass.

SKILLET. That's you son. I don't bend over and let nobody up in my booty, but I hear yo' daddy punked you for five years skraight before bein' shipped out to the state pen. Sold his own son booty for a couple of crack vials. That's penetration for *yo'* ass. *(If looks could kill from Ebony, Skillet would be buried twenty-five feet underground. This is the best check of the day. Silence for a long-ass time.)*

TOYIA. Check!

CRANK. Hell, that's five checks!

CORNBREAD. And he's the winner! *(He raises Skillet's damaged hands above his head. Everyone celebrates. Ebony seethes.)*

EBONY. You know what we do to lil' Doughboys like you?

SKILLET. Niggah, don't nobody care you second in line to the Doughboy crown round here. I might spit slow, but ain't no hoe up in me, maine. *(It's kiss or kill. A slow drone wafts from an approaching car: a song like Elvis Presley's "In the Ghetto."* Everyone freezes. While Ebony seems to grow taller, the others shrink. Crank takes Cookie by the hand and goes inside. Toyia tiptoes back into her unit. Cornbread looks down to the ground. Skillet continues to stare into Ebony's eyes. Ebony smiles.)*

EBONY. Niggah, keep on yappin'. *(To Buggy.)* You know I'm workin' for Tony C, now. *(Buggy stares at Tony C approaching.)*

BUGGY. He still round?

EBONY. Yezzir. That's a real OG for ya. *(Tony C, a forty-year-old original gangster, steps out of his Escalade all pimped out in the freshest doughboy gear. Do-rag, Ace bandages around his wrist. Bling. Wifebeater, long shorts. Tony C gives Ebony the customary hug/dap.)*

TONY C. Whassup mofo?

EBONY. Ain't nothin' much going on.

TONY C. Sorry to interrupt y'all … party — Who dis swole-ass muthafucka?

EBONY. Awww, this Buggy. You 'member him, don't it?

TONY C. If I knew him, I wouldn' be axin'.

BUGGY. I'm Big Mama grandboy.

TONY C. Yeah … I 'member you. Tiffany lil' boy. Question is, you 'member me?

BUGGY. *(Spitting on the ground.)* Yea.

TONY C. *(To Ebony.)* Glove compartment, maine. *(Ebony walks off smirking.)*

BUGGY. So you the crown round here?

TONY C. Skillet, this niggah axin' me a question? *(Skillet stays silent.)* Cornbread! *(Cornbread jumps.)* I see that house you runnin' out in South Memphis comin' 'long.

CORNBREAD. It's good. It's good.

TONY C. 'Long as you ain't got none up in *this* here complex —

CORNBREAD. Tony C, you ain't gotsta worry 'bout me. You do North Memphis, I do South … It all breezy-breezy on my end.

TONY C. Well, my boys gone need to post up on this here porch for the week. Folks gone want they goin' 'way presents. Ya feel me?

BUGGY. Ain't no need to bring this 'round my porch.

TONY C. Niggah, how this *yo'* porch?

BUGGY. I'm livin' here now.

TONY C. Yeah, well, niggah, you might live here, but you don't own this porch. *(Beat.)* Hate to hear what happened to yo' mama. Got to wonder why folk kill they self. That's usually somethin' most niggahs don't do.

BUGGY. They usually kill each other. *(Beat.)*

TONY C. *(Smiling.)* I see you done learnt somethin' in yo' lil' life. *(Shaking his head.)* How a hero gone come home to some shit like this? That's how it be for a niggah though. *(Ebony comes back and hands Tony C a package.)* Look, you a big-ass niggah. I'm lookin' for some new soljas. You need some work?

BUGGY. Work?

TONY C. I ain't stutter na'an one time now, did I, niggah? Could use somebody like you witcho skill set. You'd be a good muscle man. I bet you done kilt folks.

BUGGY. A couple.

TONY C. Me, too.

SKILLET. Me, three.

TONY C. Niggah, you ain't done shit! Shut yo' punk-ass, sissy-ass, skirt-wearin'-ass up, you slow-ass muthafucka. *(To Ebony.)* He gone get my blood pressure up.

EBONY. I know, maine. He done already got mine up. *(Tony C tries to hand Buggy a package.)*

TONY C. Take it.

BUGGY. What I'ma do wit' that?

TONY C. Take it. A lil' present. From a hustler to a hero. *(Buggy doesn't.)* Niggahs comin' back from overseas usually need to get they sniff on, smoke on. Hell, these 'Nam vets my bestus customers.

EBONY. See this shit right here, this shit right here. THIS shit righ' HERE'll take you to another muthafuckin' level, maine. Ask Funky Ricky.

TONY C. That 'Nam niggah been comin' to me for over twenty years now.

BUGGY. I don't need it. *(Beat.)*

CORNBREAD. Hell, I'll take it.

TONY C. You bet not touch that shit, you fat-ass high-yellah honkey monkey. *(Silence.)* I don't need it neither, but what I *am* needin' is a new recruit. *(To Ebony.)* You thank we could trust him?

EBONY. Tony C, he seem like a good recruit, you know what I'm sayin'? Bet he speak Iraqi and shit. Help us wit' our code —

TONY C. Niggah, what the fuck is you talkin' 'bout?

EBONY. I don't know maine. I'll be quiet.

TONY C. Yeah, niggah, why don't you do that?

BUGGY. I'll think about it.

TONY C. You know I run *all* North Memphis. I run the Hurt, Lamar Terrace, Dixie Homes, Smoky City, Scutterfield. This shit prime muthafuckin' real estate.

BUGGY. Seem like these developers thank it's prime muthafuckin' real estate, too.

TONY C. Naw, naw, soljah boy. All this shit *mine.* And don't let nobody tell you no different. *(Beat.)* I'ma be needin' somebody like you. Disciplined and shit. *(Indicating Ebony.)* Not like these other knuckleheads. Think on it. *(He snaps at Ebony, who jumps to attention. Blows a kiss to Toyia, who has come out of the unit. She nervously smiles at him. The drone dissipates as they get into their car and drive off.)*

TOYIA. I hate that song.

Scene 3

"Fleas in a Jar"

Next day. Inside of Big Mama's unit. Toyia is standing at the screen door. She ain't playin'.

TOYIA. TILAPIA! I know you ain't sittin' on my brand-new muthafuckin' Camero. I can't tell! Well, pop yo' ass right back off it then. These project kids don't know who they messin' wit. Can't wait to move up out this muthafucka. *(The television is on and music videos are playing. She begins to dance and snap her fingers to the beat.)* Oooooo! I hate this song!

27

CRANK. You hate every song BET play.

TOYIA. 'Cause I'm a muthafuckin' feminist. *(She makes her booty clap on the beat.)* "Trapped in the Closet 44" was good though. But I got that shit free from the Bootleg man, don't play. You won't catch me buyin' not a na'an 'nother R. Kelly CD. I ain't got time to be puttin' no scrilla in no pedophile's pockets. I'm a muthafuckin' feminist! Is that niggah ever gone go on trial?

CRANK. They say they waitin' 'til the girl get old enough. But wifey say she standin' by him though.

TOYIA. Awwww, hell to the naw, naw, naw! That bitch just don't wanna give up her allowance, hell, can't say I would neither, but that niggah need to be put on punishment, or somethin'. She can't let him get away with that shit. She need to put him on "pussy punishment."

CRANK. She did. That probably why he goin' around pissin' on fourteen-year-old girls.

TOYIA. Tru that!

CRANK. I heard despite it all, she 'bout to have a R. Kelly Jr.

TOYIA. Unh, unh! Wouldn't be me. Shit, "pussy punishment" the next birth control. Cornbread ain't 'bout to burn my shake junt body out. Awww, hell to the the naw, naw, naw. But the folks up at the hospital really know about pussy punishment. Folks up there had the nerve to try to tie my tubes after I had LaQwana. Nurse come over to the bed before they give me my epidural talkin' bout, "The doctor *recommends* that a woman with your *history* try a surgical approach to birth control." She might as well said, "Nigger-bitch, we don't want y'all to be havin' no mo' of y'all nigger children so we shuttin' down the reproductive power of yo' pussy!"

CRANK. Why you ain't call her out?

TOYIA. I did … I said, "Bitch, if you don't get them muthafuckin' papers out my muthafuckin' face I'ma stick a gun up in yo' muthafuckin' chest, and you won't be needin' no doctor after I'm finished witchu. You gone need a coroner." Hell, I raised the terror alert to red up in that bitch! *(They give each other high-fives.)* But she right though. I ain't got time for na'an one mo' child. And that why Cornbread on "pussy punishment." Put some red up in my head.

CRANK. Ghetto-ass.

TOYIA. Naw, bitch. I'm just expressive.

CRANK. Red weave does not look good witcho' complexion. 'Sides it's too expensive for yo' ass.

TOYIA. Hell, bitch you be jankin' it half the time. Witcho' thievin' ass.

CRANK. Hustlin'-ass. Get it right! Did Cornbread give you my money for doing yo' head these past two weeks? *(Toyia goes into her pocket and hands it to her.)*

TOYIA. *(Sucking teeth.)* You should be doin' my head for free —

CRANK. Bitch, please! *(She puts it in her bra.)* And Cornbread betta have my *other* money the next time he come up in here.

TOYIA. For what? She ain't his.

CRANK. He treat her like she is.

TOYIA. Bitch, so! Her real daddy here now, so you need go on down to that court, file them papers and get that back child support. He gone be gettin' a military check, too! Girl, don't play. You betta gone getcho own ATM — always *they* money.

CRANK. I done done good so far without him.

TOYIA. Well, get off Cornbread's dick, Miss Sojourner Truth. He already got enough to take care of — mine and then that other bitch baby out in South Memphis. You should be 'shamed of yo'-self.

CRANK. You just a jealous bitch.

TOYIA. Heifer.

CRANK. Hoe.

TOYIA. Skeezer.

CRANK. Cunt!

TOYIA. Ooooooo. I likes that one.

CRANK. That's what them British folks say. I be watchin' reruns of *Are You Being Served?*

TOYIA. Sippin' on sysyzurp?

CRANK. Naw, bitch, *Are You Being Served?*!?!?

TOYIA. What that is?

CRANK. A British TV show. I'm real culture-like.

TOYIA. How you be knowin' what them British folk be sayin'?

CRANK. Bitch, I'm just jankin' Cornbread satellite.

TOYIA. *(Under her breath.)* That ain't all you jankin'. *(Beat.)*

CRANK. Unlike you, I don't need nobody money. I gets mine own.

TOYIA. Ain't nobody done no bit of good on they own.

CRANK. How come I ain't? Ain't had to rely on not a na'an one niggah to get through. Been doin' shit on my lonesome for more than a minute. Even got clean … on my lonesome. Been clean three years now, feel me? I done done good without any man. And

29

I can do good without Buggy —

TOYIA. Can I have him then?

CRANK. NO!

TOYIA. Hell, you don't want 'em let somebody else get in where they fit in. 'Sides I be lettin' you have a taste of my Cornbread. *(Beat.)* You thank I ain't know, huh?

CRANK. Well, you be actin' like you don't want him.

TOYIA. I don't, but I want that money. He only stay around me 'cause he afraid of this back child support I'll put on his ass — which is what *you* need to be doin'.

CRANK. The baby daddy should be around for somethin' more than money, honey.

TOYIA. Maybe. Maybe not. Hell, sometimes I wonder if I hadda had my daddy. How I mighta turnt out. Shit, even if he had laid up in a corner drunk, cracked-out, watchin' TV, at least he woulda been there ya know … ya know what I'm sayin'? *(Pause.)* You know I saw him up on Auction the other day.

CRANK. What Funky Ricky doin'?

TOYIA. Same-ole, same-ole. Police had him hemmed up on a loi-terin' charge. Like he different from any other niggah standin' around on the corner all day. They 'bout to cart him off. I went up to them and say, "My daddy was waitin' on me to bring him the pamper money. Wun't no loiterin'. Just waitin' up on Auction." They took one look at me let him go. Like they expected me to have a cracked-out daddy like that. I couldn' believe that shit came out my mouth. He ain't never said "that my daughter." Niggah, ain't even recognize me. Hmph … That lil' girl daddy here. Let her have that. Be grateful. Ain't shit wrong wit' 'em. He ain't no Funky Ricky. He seem a lil' white boy actin' sometime, but he always been that way. He ain't a total bastard.

CRANK. He ain't come back for me. Fuck that niggah.

TOYIA. At least he done come back.

CRANK. She look just like 'em.

TOYIA. Spittin' muthafuckin' image. Got his teeth. His attitude, his … *(Crank is visibly agitated. She starts throwing her cosmetology tools in their plastic containers. Toyia notices.)* Look, bitch, like I say, put that niggah on child support, get them military benefits 'cause I'm tired of you takin' my money. *And* you can get you a lil' dick on the side, too, then maybe you'll stop bein' so fuckin' cranky. *(Cookie enters through the screen door carrying a Mason jar. She goes straight to the back room to put her backpack up.)*

CRANK. What, you gone come up in this house and not speak?

COOKIE. *(From offstage.)* Hey.

TOYIA. Chillun just ain't got no kinds of manners nowadays, but I wouldn't say hey to yo' ass neither if you was my mama. *(Crank pulls her hair tight with a comb.)* Ouch! *(Cookie comes back in.)*

COOKIE. They gave us a science project for the first week. I don't know how to do it.

TOYIA. Don't look at me. I'm a puredee fool.

CRANK. You'll figure it out, Cookie.

COOKIE. I need some money for da posta board.

TOYIA. You betta take one of them boxes, cut it up, and let that be the end of it, shee-it.

COOKIE. But folk gone be comin' to school wit' dat nice posterboard.

CRANK. 'Cause they come from folk who can waste money on buyin' stupid shit like that. Like Toyia say, cut up one of them boxes and call it a day. What this is anyway?

COOKIE. Fleas in a jar.

CRANK. What in a jar!?!?

COOKIE. It's fleas in a jar!

TOYIA. I know you ain't brought no fleas up in here. Y'all already got roaches. Them niggahs gone breed and become fleoches.

COOKIE. That ain't gone happen.

TOYIA. Watch!

CRANK. What the hell this for?

COOKIE. Science class. I gotta test my hypothesis.

TOYIA. Hypothewhat? Is that the new project baby name? I need to write that down.

COOKIE. Hypothesis! You gotta have an educated guess about yo' project. It mean, like, you guess how it gone turn out.

TOYIA. Okay, whatcho hiphopcracy?

COOKIE. *(Rolling her eyes.)* Right now, the fleas keep on jumpin' up and they keep hittin' they head, right? Look. *(They crowd around the Mason jar.)*

TOYIA. Sho' nuff is.

COOKIE. Afterwhile, they gone realize that if they jump so high, they gone ram they head into the lid.

CRANK. Unh, hunh ...

COOKIE. So, it's nine fleas up in there now. Well, after 'bout a week the fleas stop jumpin' so high 'cause they know they gone bump they head. That's when you take off the lid. The fleas could jump out but because they done got tired of hurtin' theyself they won't jump no higher than the lid. Ain't nothin' holdin' them in, but they thank so. I bet if I leave the lid off, it'll still be nine fleas in there at the end of the week 'cause they ain't gone jump high enough to get out.

CRANK. Sound like some shit to me. *(Beat.)*

COOKIE. I'm just testin' it out.

CRANK. And yo' lil' smart tail testin' me. Gone to yo' room and do yo' homework.

COOKIE. But I need help wit' it. They want me to write a report —

CRANK. Git! *(Just then, Buggy and Cornbread enter the unit.)*

CORNBREAD. What, you actin' up again?

CRANK. She back talkin' as usual.

COOKIE. No, I ain't.

CORNBREAD. Ay, girl, don't be back talkin' yo' mama.

COOKIE. Shut up! You ain't my daddy! Unfortunately, he is. I hate all y'all! *(She stands in the doorway of the back room, sulking.)*

CRANK. Talkin' 'bout she need some help. She need to learn how not to axe nobody for no help. She need to learn how to depend on herself.

BUGGY. If the girl need help, help her.

CRANK. Why don't you help her then Mr. Smartypants I-done-went-to-the-military-and-I-know-everythang-God-know-and-then some?

BUGGY. Awww, I forgot you wun't too good on homework back-in-the-day.

CRANK. I could help her if I wanted to.

BUGGY. You don't even know how to help yo'self. Cookie, I'll help you wit' it.

COOKIE. Really?

BUGGY. Yeah. We can do it later on. *(Crank stares the smiling Cookie down, who shrinks beneath her mother's gaze. Big Mama enters from the back room rushing around. She is putting on her custodian outfit.)*

BIG MAMA. This night shift is gone run me damn near crazy.

CRANK. You is late as a mug.

BIG MAMA. Who you tellin'? *(Mumbling to herself.)* I can't never find shit round here. I'm supposeta be down there now. It's a Friday night. Gone be a lot of niggah blood to mop up. What, the boys ain't gone go on down to Beale Street? I hear somethin' goin' on down at the Pyramid.

TOYIA. Cornbread on punishment.

CORNBREAD. Bitch, you don't run me.

TOYIA. Niggah, you betta watch how you speak to me. See, just for that, I'm adding three more days to the pussy strike!

BIG MAMA. Can't find my ortho' shoes …

BUGGY. Let me help ya.

BIG MAMA. Crank, you pack up my shoes?

CRANK. Naw, I don't know where they at.

BIG MAMA. Oh, Lord, I need to get out of here. Y'all heifers always holdin' me up!

BUGGY. I'll help you find it, Big Mama.

BIG MAMA. Prolly in these boxes right here. Help me go through this goddamn thang. *(They go over to a box. Buggy lifts it and as he does the bottom falls out.)* Goddamn it! Crank, clean this shit up! *(Out has tumbled a red pair of platform heels and other various hooker clothes.)*

COOKIE. Ohhh, weee, these so pretty … *(Cookie goes to pick up the red shoes. Big Mama slaps her on the behind, and turns her around.)*

BIG MAMA. Don't you ever put yo' feet up in a dead woman's shoes. You hear me? You liable to walk out yo' life the same way she did. *(Beat.)*

BUGGY. These was my mama's favorite shoes.

BIG MAMA. Well, you ain't got no favorites when you gone. *(Beat.)*

TOYIA. Here they go, Big Mama. *(Toyia hands Big Mama's shoes from under the couch.)*

BIG MAMA. Where was you hidin' these? In yo' cooch?

TOYIA. Big Mama, if you don't get yo' butt on to work …

BIG MAMA. How come I'm the only one goin' to work? *(They all look their separate ways. Silence.)* Y'all a cryin' shame.

33

Scene 4

"Poppin' Pills"

Nighttime. Sweat. The crunk drone bass from passing cars leaks into the unit from outside. Cookie is tiptoeing in the darkness trying not to wake up Buggy, who is tossing and turning on the couch. Then gunshots pop off, shattering the night. Buggy wakes up with a start as if he had been submerged under water about to drown. He seems to break through the surface for a gulp of air.

BUGGY. Mama!? Mama!?

COOKIE. Naw, dawg. It yo' lil' mama.

BUGGY. What the hell you doin' up?

COOKIE. Shhhhhhh! Fo' you wake e'erbody up. I done peed in the bed. Need to change them sheets.

BUGGY. Too much information.

COOKIE. Well you axed! *(Pop. Pow. Pow. Gunshots echo.)*

BUGGY. Do these niggahs ever go to sleep?

COOKIE. They don't like to dream.

BUGGY. Naw, they don't like to have nightmares.

COOKIE. You sweatin' hard.

BUGGY. Goddamn plastic on this couch make a muthafucka feel like he up in a sauna.

COOKIE. Air conditioner prolly broke right before you went to sleep. Everythang always be breakin' round here. *(She pours him some water out of the refrigerator.)*

BUGGY. On the real though. Pass me my duffel. *(She does. Buggy digs into his bag and pulls out a bottle of pills. His hands are shaking uncontrollably. He's having trouble opening it. Cookie takes it from him and easily twists off the top. Laughing it off.)* These things supposed to be child proof.

COOKIE. I ain't no chile.

BUGGY. Not no more. *(He seems to see himself in her for the first time. He gulps down the water. She picks up his medicine bottles.)*

34

COOKIE. Norpramin … Paxil …

BUGGY. You can read?

COOKIE. Hell, yeah I can read!

BUGGY. Well, keep on. Stay in school. Go to college.

COOKIE. How 'bout I go into the military witchu?

BUGGY. No need.

COOKIE. I can get a scholarship, can't I?

BUGGY. You watch too much TV.

COOKIE. Naw, that what them recruits up at the mall be sayin'.

BUGGY. At the mall? Hmmph.

COOKIE. She hit me when I pee in the bed.

BUGGY. You can't control that shit.

COOKIE. Yeah, but I can't buy no new mattress neither.

BUGGY. What you wanna be when you grow up?

COOKIE. What this bullshit is? Catchup time? *(Beat.)* A rapper.

BUGGY. Why don't you become a doctor?

COOKIE. E'er niggah ain't gotsta be a Huxtable. Rappin' gone be my side hustle. 'Sides, I really wanna be a flight attendant. *(Buggy laughs at her.)* You sittin' over there laughin', but when I'm flyin' in the friendly skies e'erbody gone be axin' me for a ticket. I heard you can go anywhere you wanna. I'd go, maine … I'd'n know where I'd go, but I'd fly far away … *(Beat.)* I take pills, too. Birth control.

BUGGY. You don't need to be fuckin' already.

COOKIE. You wanna come up in here and be my daddy now, huh? I don't see it though. I don't look nothin' like you.

BUGGY. You might not be mine for all I know.

COOKIE. You'd like that now wouldn't you?

BUGGY. You just like yo' mama.

COOKIE. Yeah, that's what they say. What was you dreamin' 'bout? *(Beat.)*

BUGGY. That I was driving in my Humvee over there. Regular mornin'. I'm rollin' through a quiet hood. Look just like ours but real peaceful like. Smilin'. I'm bumpin' a lil' Kanye West —

COOKIE. Kanye West for faggots —

BUGGY. Okay, Jay-Z —

COOKIE. Mmmmmmm.

BUGGY. Wu-Tang?

COOKIE. *(High-pitched.)* MMMMMMM.

BUGGY. 8 Ball and MJG? Three 6 Mafia?

COOKIE. THASS betta —

BUGGY. On the speaker. All of a sudden this fire ball come up from between my legs. Roadside bomb. Next thing I know, I'm lookin' down at my body. Well, half of it. My top half blew out the Humvee and hit the road. All my guts just spilled out into the dirt below my belly button. Eyes rolled up into the back of my head. All you could see was the white of my eyes, like I never had no color in them.

COOKIE. Sound like muthafuckin' *Platoon* or some shit.

BUGGY. Yo' mama let you watch that?

COOKIE. Naw. Peaches 'nem be stealin' cable, too. See it over there. *(Beat.)* What was his name?

BUGGY. Lieutenant Michael Bond.

COOKIE. Y'all was close? *(He nods his head.)* Be grateful that shit ain't happen to you. Do they make it go away? *(She points to the pills.)*

BUGGY. Naw … Some things you just can't get over. *(Cookie takes a pill and pops it into her mouth. She chews it like candy.)*

COOKIE. I have.

Scene 5

"America Ain't Shit"

The unit. Next day. Cookie is playing with her dollhouse in the corner. She is acting out a play with her dolls.

COOKIE. *(Male voice.)* "Oh, Princess Tequila Alizé Jenkins will you throw down your hair so I can climb up and take you away? *(Female voice.)* "Honey, this weave glued in, not sewed. You liable to pull out a patch of my hair you climb up like that! How 'bout I get you a rope?" *(Male voice.)* "Bitch, you betta just send down that weave. I ain't got time — "

CRANK. *(Offstage.)* COOKIE!!!

COOKIE. What!

CRANK. *(Offstage.)* Why it smell like piss in this back room?

COOKIE. I don't know what you talkin' 'bout … *(Crank comes into the room.)*

CRANK. You do know what I'm talkin' 'bout.

COOKIE. It might be Big Mama. You know how old folk be peein' in the bed —

CRANK. Don't you lie to me, nah!

COOKIE. I ain't tellin' no story.

CRANK. She ain't that old to be peein' in the bed.

COOKIE. I read it in a book. Folks wit' diabetes pee a lot. 'Specially in the mornin'. *(Beat.)*

CRANK. For real? You ain't lyin'?

COOKIE. Swear fo' God …

CRANK. I guess we gone need to get that bitch some Depends, then. *(Cookie starts giggling. Crank starts laughing, too. Beat.)* You finish yo' homework?

COOKIE. Yeah.

CRANK. You want me to check it?

COOKIE. Uh. No.

CRANK. How come?

COOKIE. 'Cause … you know … we doin' seventh-grade stuff.

CRANK. Like what?

COOKIE. English stuff … you know?

CRANK. Well, I can speak English.

COOKIE. It just grammar questions … I can check over it myself.

CRANK. Just let me see it. *(A hesitant Cookie goes into her backpack. She gives it to her. Crank looks at it, blankly.)* That good.

COOKIE. It's all correct?

CRANK. Mmmmhmmm. From what I see. *(Crank hands it back to her. Cookie inspects it.)*

COOKIE. Ma, the first one wrong.

CRANK. No it ain't. I looked at it.

COOKIE. But it's wrong. I put down that it was a adjective and it a adverb.

CRANK. What, you think I'm lyin'? That's right.

COOKIE. No, it ain't. It ain't! *(Crank smacks Cookie in the back of her head.)* I'ma tell Big Mama!

CRANK. Tell her! I'm 'bout tireda you callin' me a lie!

COOKIE. But you is. You can't read.

CRANK. What, you thank I'm stupid? I ain't stupid. I'm like Maya Angelou up in this bitch, I'm a muthafuckin' genius. You get it from ya mama!

COOKIE. I shoulda got Daddy to check my homework! *(Beat.)*

CRANK. "Daddy"? Since when he become "Daddy" allasudden. *(Crank grabs her by the collar.)* Listen you lil' bitch, I'm yo' mammy, yo' daddy, yo' God, yo' everything. You bet not call him Daddy again. If you do, I'ma get that electric cord … Believe that playa. *(Big Mama bursts through the door and surveys the room.)*

BIG MAMA. WHY Y'ALL AIN'T FINISHED PACKIN'? I TOLD Y'ALL LIL' BITCHES WE NEED TO BE PACKED UP BY THE END OF THE WEEK. HOW COME NOBODY LISTEN TO ME? I JUST DON'T UNDERSTAND IT! NOBODY LISTEN TO ME. *(Crank lets go of Cookie.)*

COOKIE. We gone pack it all up, I promise, it'll all be done, damn …

CRANK. I just finished packin' all my boxes today. They say them men gone be here come tomorrow to give us some mo' boxes — *(Big Mama goes on a tirade around the apartment.)*

BIG MAMA. Cookie take that damn dollhouse in the back fo' I burn it. This food ain't packed up yet? Y'all just ain't gone listen to me, huh? Gotta tell y'all somethin' nine or ten times 'fo' ya listen. WHY NOBODY EVER LISTEN! *(Big Mama throws a bottle against the wall. It shatters. Silence.)* We ain't goin' nowhere. *(Silence. She means it.)* Them cracker-ass muthafuckas. If it ain't one thang it's another. I done worked hard all my life and this what they give me. Been to hell and back on wheels of fire and a seat of stone and what I got to show for it? Four raggedy-ass boxes and a toe-up-to-the-flo'-up-ass JC Penney catalog full of check marks next to shit I ain't gone never be able to afford.

COOKIE. Big Mama, whass wrong?

BIG MAMA. They actin' like they ain't gone put us up. Sayin' I'm makin' too much for the Section 8 housin' out in Raleigh. Wit' my lil' rinky-dink job over there at the V.A.? Say our application done got "denied." Now we ain't got nowhere to move come next Friday — and WHY MY MUTHAFUCKIN' 'FRIGERATOR DON'T WORK! *(She kicks it, stubs her toe.)* Lawd, when it rain it pour. I make 387 dollars over. 387 dollars put me o'er the limit and they say it gone take two months for a appeal! 387 dollars? Well … I ain't goin' nowhere. I'ma chain myself to this bitch 'cause they can't tear it down wit' me in it. Tell anybody who axe. Instead a crackin' down on Welfare they need to crack down on how many of them knuckleheads out there killin' folks. How lil' girls go outside to play and get snatched up by some rapist. They don't care about that. White folk always care about the wrong damn thang.

CRANK. What 'bout yo' sister in the burbs? Don't she got a house out in Davies Plantation?

BIG MAMA. Niggahs done fought to get off the plantation, and here this bitch done fought tooth and nail to get back on it. Fuck her. She the most selfish bitch I done ever knownt.

COOKIE. Big Mama, am I still gone be able to go to that school?

BIG MAMA. Cookie, ain't nobody worried 'bout that right nah! First we gotsta make sho' a roof gone be over our heads come next week. We gone have to scrape up some money or us 'n' our boxes gone be out on the skreet. Livin' paycheck to paycheck and this shit up 'n' happen. I'ma have to go on down to the Welfare office. I can't stand goin' down to that office. *(Buggy enters — a bit jittery.)* Where you been?

BUGGY. Off.

BIG MAMA. I sees that much …

CRANK. These white folk tryin' to do something horrible. We ain't got nowhere to move. Say we makin' too much money to live on Section 8. *(She tries to read the letter.)* "You have ex — cee — ded the a — " *(Cookie takes the paper out of her hand.)*

COOKIE. " — llotment for the head of household."

BIG MAMA. Well, at least my Buggy done come home. We can go live with him. Military take care of housin', ain't that the truth of it? We can just live off the military check he gone get.

BUGGY. Uhhm —

CRANK. You done come in the nick of time.

BIG MAMA. I know that's right. Now, we ain't gone have to scramble, but if you calls yo' lieutenant or the military or whoever we can be moved in somewhere by next Friday.

BUGGY. That ain't the way it work.

BIG MAMA. How come it don't?

CRANK. Well, how it work? We'll do what we gotta do to make it work.

BUGGY. What y'all need to do, you ain't gone never do.

CRANK. I'll do it with the quickness.

BUGGY. The guvment ain't gotsta give you nothin.'

BIG MAMA. I can't tell!

BUGGY. The city ain't gone have y'all livin' out on the streets. There are shelters.

BIG MAMA. I ain't gone live in no muthafuckin' shelta.

BUGGY. Look at where you stayin' at, Big Mama. Look at this muthafuckin' hole! Hell, a shelta a lot betta than this.

BIG MAMA. Them folk don't care nothin' 'bout us. They want us dead.

BUGGY. Hell, "they" ain't got to care 'bout you, and who the fuck is "they"? "They." "They." Where "they" hiding at? I ain't never seen't no "they." "They" is you and you and you. "They" is them niggahs runnin' 'round outside sittin' around and ain't got shit else to do. That's who "they" is!

BIG MAMA. Oh, you just done went to wherever and got all sid-dity on a niggah, ain't ya?

BUGGY. Naw, Big Mama. I'm just callin' it how I see it. It ain't no "they." You right. "They" don't care about us. "They" ain't got to care. And I ain't none of "they." I do care. If I had it, I would give it, but I can't and not 'cause I won't but cuz I don't got. I don't got, Big Mama.

CRANK. Don't they give y'all a monthly check or is that the navy?

BIG MAMA. I tolja ya shoulda went into da navy.

CRANK. Yeah, I think it's the navy that give you a check.

BUGGY. That ain't the way it work!!!!

BIG MAMA. But folks down at the V.A. say —

BUGGY. FUCK THEM MUTHAFUCKAS AT THE V.A. I just been down there and they can't help me!

BIG MAMA. What you mean they can't help —

BUGGY. Folks like me can't be helped —

CRANK. Then what we supposedta do? *(Buggy begins to tremble uncontrollably.)* You need to be the man of the house. You got a daughter that need to be took care of. Big Mama need to be took care of and I need to be took care of.

BUGGY. I need my medicine. I need. I need my med —

CRANK. What the hell's wrong witchu!

BIG MAMA. Buggy …

BUGGY. I needs my medication. I need it … I need my pills — *(Cookie drops her doll house at the sight of it all. It makes a huge crashing noise. Buggy dives behind the boxes like a scared little boy. He is breathing hard and deeply from the bottom of his belly.)* We been hit. Skywalker 16 been hit. Attack grid coordinate MB 4-3-0-6-8-niner-7-niner. DANGER CLOSE. Fire comin' over the sand dune west. We hit. Hit, hit, hit, hit … hit … hit … hit … hi …

hii ... hii ... hi ... h ... h ... h. *(Silence. Cookie walks over to her father. She reaches out to comfort, but her small hands startle him. For a second he doesn't know who she is. Once he realizes, he breaks down into tears, slouching against the boxes.)*

BIG MAMA. Don't no military check come in the mail for folk like him. I done seen this down at the V.A. Call it "*other* than honorable discharge." Call it "niggah crazy." I'm old enough to know betta. America ain't shit.

ACT TWO

Scene 1

"Tony C's Emancipation Proclamation"

Outside the units. "The Hurt Village is falling down" refrain is heard lightly in the background. In front of the spray-painted wall that says "Das Haus des jammers," Skillet and Ebony are smoking on a huge blunt.

EBONY. I don't even know what that shit say.

SKILLET. Niggah, 'cause you can't read.

EBONY. Niggah, I passed the fifth grade three times. Bet. "Those hoes bes jammin'!" See there.

SKILLET. That ain't it.

EBONY. Alright then, niggah. You decode the ghetto hieroglyphics.

SKILLET. Can't. 'Cause I'm HIgh as a MUFUCKA, maine!

EBONY. Niggah, how come you ain't tell me you had more weed?

SKILLET. You know how weed make you forget; I forgot. Speakin' a which, I forgot to tell you. This niggah down by the Pyramid gone axe me, which one I rather have. Pussy or weed? I say, "Niggah? Now what kind of question is that?" I'm the type a niggah, can't live without neither, but I much rather have some weed than some pussy.

EBONY. Niggah, you gay-ass-faggot-ass-bitch-ass-niggah —

SKILLET. Naw, niggah … hear me out. Pussy and weed … got some similarities. Pussy and weed taste good … when they wet.

EBONY. What bitch done let yo' ugly ass eat her out?

SKILLET. Yo' mammy, niggah — now listen! — they both … got a distinct smell. They both can have … you happy and give you the munchies 'til six o'clock in the morning. They both can burn ya' if you get too close to the tip. They both can turn yo' lips black, you suck on it too much. See, I likes 'em both, but …

pussy leave you. Weed don't care nothin' 'bout yo' job, yo' credit or yo' car. Weed'll chill witcha … anywhere and nowhere. Make everything real … slow … motion like. Pussy speed shit up: the decreasement of the gas in yo' tank, yo' bank account, and yo' … beloved weed.

EBONY. I like 'em when they both together. Now, I done seen a pussy smoke some weed.

SKILLET. Run tell that!

EBONY. This girl down at Pure Passion put a blunt up in her chocha and smoked it. Swear 'fo' God!

SKILLET. Hell muthafuckin' yeah! That's my next 'speriment. I can make pussy-smellin' weed!

EBONY. Hell, don't nobody wanna come back home smellin' like weed and pussy. It either one or the other. Yo' girl sho' to put ya out on the humble if you come back smellin' like both. But you wouldn't know nathan 'bout that no way.

SKILLET. Naw, dawg, I'm on a marketing grind: "Pussy weed." Niggahs'll eat that shit up, you know what I'm sayin'?
    Gotta make that money cuz
    I gotta get my own place
    Can't stay wit' my cousin no mo'
    Gotta go. Gotta go
    I stay high on the ya-yo —
    Jump the boogie
    Woulja puff puff pass that pussy to me.

EBONY. To me! *(They laugh.)* You a stupid-ass niggah.

SKILLET. That was brilliant. I'ma have ta record that … Three Six Mafia could use that verse.

EBONY. That shit's whack, niggah! I ain't never heard nothin' like that in my life. No wonder Tony C don't give you no work.

SKILLET. Bet! Niggahs buy all kinds of pussy on the corner anyway. Hell, let 'em buy mine. *(Cookie comes out of her unit.)*

BIG MAMA. *(Offstage.)* Make sure you bring back two beers. Colt 45. In a can. No bottles. 'Cause I'm liable to break it off in somebody face. Yo' daddy need one and I need one. Take yo' ass down to the liquor sto' and bring yo' ass skraight on back. Gone, nah. *(Cookie walks down the street.)*

EBONY. That little bitch look like she gone be finer than her mama.

SKILLET. Maine, she stout as a mug already, maine.

EBONY. She not too light, not too dark neither. Just that right kinda brown, niggah. That shit right there, THAT shit right there, that right THERE must be tight.

SKILLET. I like her mind. *(Ebony smacks him upside the head. Cookie glares at them then jiggles the change in her pockets as she skips along.)*

SKILLET and EBONY. Hey, Cookie! *(There is the sound of music coming from a car in the distance. Beep. Beep. The car horn goes. The boys scatter and run. BEEP. BEEP.)*

TONY C. Look, silly-ass girl. You see I'm tryin' to talk to you. *(She keeps walking.)* Ay, Cookie! *(Cookie stops.)* Come over here. *(Cookie stays where she is. Tony's car door slams. He walks up to her.)* "It's a beautiful day in the neighborhood, a beautiful day for you neightbor. Won't you be mine? Won't you be mine?"

COOKIE. Hell, naw.

TONY C. Whassup lil' playa. You headed to get a pickle from the candylady?

COOKIE. Naw, a beer.

TONY C. Damn, that bitch sell beer now.

COOKIE. Naw, she done moved out already. I'm goin' to the liquor sto'.

TONY C. Ride wit' me. I'll take you down there. *(Silence.)* I respect that. I guess we gone be neighbors since y'all movin' out to Raleigh.

COOKIE. Ain't nobody movin' out to Raleigh.

TONY C. Why not?

COOKIE. Crackers. I bet you got a big-ass house out in Raleigh.

TONY C. Four bedroom, two full bath, a living room —

COOKIE. *And* a dinin' room?

TONY C. A businessman always need a muthafuckin' dinin' room for his guests.

COOKIE. You got a extra room? *(Silence.)*

TONY C. Naw, I got my moms, my sis and her four kids, my four wit' me at the crib. Ain't no mo' room at the inn, lil' bit.

COOKIE. City say we make too much for help.

TONY C. That good, ain' it?

COOKIE. Hell, naw.

TONY C. The city know they stay pullin' that shit. Learn this befo' you learn anythan' else. Crackers ain't gone give you shit. You gots to take it. That's one thang niggahs ain't never learnt, yet. Not stealin', but takin'. Like we got a niggah mayor right — muthafuckin' Mayor Willie Herenton, right. But it's all fo' show 'cause that niggah don't care nothin' 'bout you or me. He gettin' boocoo bank from the guvment to "revitalize" these here projects. Millions! Movin' niggahs out like Hebrews to make room for who?

COOKIE. Crackers!

TONY C. Thass right, niece! City use the guvment money to bull-doze this shit, then these private developers gone swoop in like roaches to rice, gettin' prime muthafuckin' real estate for free. End of the day Lil' Willie, this South Memphis – lookin'-ass niggah, gettin' paid millions to get paid more on the back end. 'Cause you know they just gone build some condos and Hurt Village niggahs ain't gone be able to 'ford that shit! It's a muthafuckin' conspiracy up in this bitch. He too busy makin' *his* dough, *his* paper. Hell, I shoulda been the mayor! But thass the politickin' of the projects, pure and simple. Getcho shit together, you gotsta always be on yo' job. See these Chink-ass mofos they got liquo' sto'es and check-cashin' sto'es takin' twenty dollars out cho' check to give you yo' money.

COOKIE. I know that's right.

TONY C. What kinda sense that make? What we got? Nathan! They make the money and take that shit out to wherever they at. We all gettin' fucked in the ass over here, niece. We all gettin' raped. But you got to get in where you fit in. Hell, I know my place. I sell that white to these niggahs so my lil' boy won't ever have to play on a playground got mo' crack vials than blades of grass. I'll be damned that happen. I'll be damned. So … if I gotsta kill a couple niggahs who was on they way out anyway, so be it. It's for the greater good. *(Beat.)* Fuck Section 8. They was gone put y'all on the bad side of Raleigh anyway. Can you add?

COOKIE. Yeah.

TONY C. Subtract?

COOKIE. Betta.

TONY C. Lil' niggahs always betta at losin' than gainin'. You wanna be my lil' friend?

COOKIE. If you stop playin' Elvis …

TONY C. Y'all lil' niggahs don't know nuthin' 'bout good music. Elvis grew up round the Hurt. *(Off of her reaction of surprise.)* Ye'en know? These projects was built for white folks. Wun't no niggahs stayin' round here in the fifties. Just kikes, Polacks, wops, I don't know the bad name you use for Germans — ginks. Whatever. I bet they don't teach you that at school. Now, Elvis that's the original

American idol. Came right from round the Hurt. I like his philosophy, too. The only thing a niggah can do for me is shine my shoes and buy my shit, too —

BUGGY. Cookie, come on in this house. *(Buggy has come out of the unit onto the porch. She doesn't move.)* Cookie, I ain't gotta say it again, do I? *(Cookie smiles. He means business.)*

COOKIE. I ain't went to get the beer yet.

BUGGY. Well, carry yo' ass on and be back quick fast. *(She skips away.)*

TONY C. She a real sweet girl. You shoulda had named her after yo' mama. "Tiffany" a pretty girl name. You think 'bout what I toldja?

BUGGY. Stay 'way from her.

TONY C. Can't. She too precious.

BUGGY. I got a gun. I know how to use it.

TONY C. Whoa! Slow yo' roll, solja boy. Me, too, ye'en know?

BUGGY. I ain't gone tell you again.

TONY C. Done come back to the cut and wanna shoot up e'erything in sight. Be grateful you can walk skraight. Gotcho senses about cha. I said, did you think about what I told you?

BUGGY. I ain't sellin' shit for you. I ain't gone sell this shit period.

TONY C. Wha? The buck-ass business man gone? Just a lil' solja boy ra-pa-pummin' in his place. Where the fuck yo' drum?

BUGGY. Right here. Who axin'?

TONY C. A maine. A maine that's proud of one of the Hurt's finest soldiers. You coulda been like me.

BUGGY. But, I ain't you.

TONY C. You right 'bout that: You ain't. You too "good." You'll never be a Kang like me.

BUGGY. I don't wanna see you round this here porch again. *(Beat. Big Mama emerges behind the screen door and she stares at Tony C. He smiles.)*

TONY C. And the boy comes back a man. *(Tony C walks away into the dusk. From the far distance shots echo. Big Mama comes out on the porch and sits on the rickety, rusty metal chair.)*

BIG MAMA. You got a Kool on you?

BUGGY. I thought you only smoked Parliaments?

BIG MAMA. I ain't got no Parliament money, so give me a muthafuckin' Kool. Ain't no rest for the weary. You a'ight?

BUGGY. As a'ight as a crazy man can be.

BIG MAMA. You ain't crazy.

BUGGY. I'ma be crazy if I don't get me no more pills. Niggahs down at the V.A. —

BIG MAMA. What they say when you went down there?

BUGGY. That they can't refill me no more. I'm on my last script … Spend ten years goin' everywhere they tell you to go, doin' e'erthang they tell you to do. You make one mistake — ONE mistake and — they just kick you out.

BIG MAMA. Well, what you do?

BUGGY. Nothin' nobody else ain't do.

BIG MAMA. Naw, but what *you* do? *(Silence.)* Well … that's how they do our boys. They use 'em for what they need, then throw 'em away when they done. Like a man fuckin' a hoe for free. It's all old hat wit' me.

BUGGY. I'm right back where I started. Worser off to boot. Can't get my benefits. Ain't gone be able to get no job. A bad conduct discharge like a damn felony for a niggah they sayin'. And I thought these stars and bars was gone set me free. Hell, maybe I should go work for Tony C.

BIG MAMA. Naw, naw, Buggy, you bigger than that.

BUGGY. I can't have us livin' out on the streets. Y'all right. I got to take care of you, Cookie, then there's Crank —

BIG MAMA. You was surprised to see her wun't ya?

BUGGY. Yeah, but I was glad. Real glad you took her in.

BIG MAMA. Only reason I let Crank stay is 'cause she look just like ya mama. Beautiful girl ain't she? Would be mo' pretty if she just smile a lil' bit mo'. Had a bit of happiness in her heart. She did what yo' mama couldn't do. Quit. She woulda been forty years old this week. Tiffany woulda been forty years old …

BUGGY. It's my fault mama died, Big Mama. I was the one brought that shit into the house. One day Mama took it and she took it all. I 'member her layin' on the bathroom floor, and I went to get a blanket 'cause I thought she was cold. She wun't cold. She was dead.

BIG MAMA. Ain't no use in blamin' yo'self. Yo mammy was a fuckin' crackhead. She was my daughter, but she was a crackhead. Plain and simple. Hell, some time I wonder if I wasn't so hard on her. Maybe she woulda done right eventually. If I hadna hit on her so much. If I hadna yelled at her … But coulda, woulda, shoulda give you gray hair and I'm too fine to be havin' some gray hair. Besides, you can't cry over spilt milk.

47

BUGGY. Spilt blood different. *(Beat.)* I might have to sell. Big Mama. One last time. *(Big Mama pulls her letter out.)*
BIG MAMA. Three hundred eighty-seven dollars … We niggahs on the cusp. Not too po' not too rich.
BUGGY. Maybe this a good thang to not hafta rely on nobody but yo'self. Do for yo'self. All fo' yo'self. We might can do it. If I just sell a lil' bit …
BIG MAMA. I know … I know. I'll get you some gloves from the hospital. The Hurt ain't changed a bit.

Scene 2

"The Last Shipment"

Cornbread's unit on the upper level. Their hands covered with surgical gloves, Buggy and Cornbread are in the kitchen cooking crack. Buggy pours baking soda into a boiling pot.

CORNBREAD. Niggah, that's too much!
BUGGY. Niggah, that ain't enough!
CORNBREAD. You gone buy me some mo' bakin' soda you keep on dumpin' it in the pot like it's water!
BUGGY. How you gone turn a profit if you don't really cut the shit?
CORNBREAD. Look, my shit be pure. I got customers been comin' to me for ten years. *(Cornbread looks at his concoction boiling on the stove.)* I'ma make 'bout 100 cookies on this shit. And some pancakes at that.
BUGGY. How much you thank we make?
CORNBREAD. We?
BUGGY. Yeah, niggah, we …
CORNBREAD. At least two thou. Easy. In a week. Especially if … we run it together out in North *and* South Memphis. Hell, maybe sell it in the Hurt.
BUGGY. Tony C wouldn't like that …
CORNBREAD. Hell, Toyia pocketbook would. So … whatchoo gone do, niggah? You gone run this wit' me or what? *(Beat.)*

48

BUGGY. One last time.

CORNBREAD. That's what I'm talkin' 'bout niggah! We run that. Like we used to do. Like we used to DO! I get these last couple of crates from my distributor dude, then I'll be out.

BUGGY. Who you get yo' distribution from nah?

CORNBREAD. These Vietnamese niggahs live out over in Scutterfield. They shit be on that purdee white. *(He takes a lighter and burns it for Buggy.)*

BUGGY. Clearer than Tony C shit be.

CORNBREAD. He get his shit from them Mexicans off Jackson, but them Chinks make the besto crackos!

BUGGY. We chop this shit up nice and clear make the money we need to make.

CORNBREAD. And be out!

BUGGY. And don't violate Biggie crack commandment number four —

BUGGY and CORNBREAD. "Never get high on yo' own supply!" *(They laugh.)*

CORNBREAD. Only drug go up in me is a lil' bit of purple. And the Indians did that shit so it must be good for ya.

BUGGY. That's that quarter Cherokee in you talkin'.

CORNBREAD. I'm everythang and nothin' at all. *(They laugh like old buds.)*

BUGGY. I owe you. You takin' care of Cookie like she yo' own and shit.

CORNBREAD. Yeah, you do. I ain't mind raisin' her like she was my own. Always feel good to step in yo' shoes. Even for a lil' while. *(Beat. Cornbread stirs up the crack pot on the stove.)* Hell, we make mo' than I thank, I just might stay up in it. The Hurt might be lookin' at a new Kang afterwhile. Kang Cornbread, how that sound!

BUGGY. I thought this yo' last shipment?

CORNBREAD. Yeah, yeah, but thank about it? Me 'n' you together? We could quite possibly take over. They might be tearin' down the Hurt, but it's some mo' muthafuckin' places, maine. Build us up a empire. We could be partners, partnah! We can have our house in the 'burbs and come check on our crackhouses in the projects. That's real breezy-breezy fo' me. Too bad you goin' back overseas maine. That'd be the dream wouldn't it?

BUGGY. If I stayed … we would need more than me and you to do the do.

CORNBREAD. Pull in Skillet. Pull in a lotta these lil' niggahs, maine. We could push Tony C out of North Memphis! Take over that Million Dollar Track. Do what we do. You can't run from who you is niggah.

BUGGY. Sho'll can't. Sho'll can't.

CORNBREAD. Ooooooo 'member when we was just lil' hustlers, wun't nothin' 'bout fourteen years old? We was walkin' under the train tracks on Lauderdale Skreet and ran into Tony C Auction Skreet Hustlers. We was some lil'-ass skinny-ass niggahs then, maine. And one of them muthafuckas threw a bottle down hit me in the face. Niggah lucky it ain't leave a scar on my pretty-ass face. I'm cryin', but you ran after them mofos, yoked 'em up. They ain't come after us no' mo'. You ain't scared of nathan, maine. You was everybody hero after that, maine. You always get boocoo respect. I bet a hero like you, gets plenty respect over there maine. *(Buggy laughs uncomfortably.)*

BUGGY. Respect? Cornbread ... I done did some thangs to the point where ... I ain't gone be goin' back over there. You right. I ain't changed. Seem like the mo' I tried to run away from who I is the mo' it follow me. Death for a niggah is everywhere. Whether you in the projects or on the battlefield. Ain't no escapin' what God got for ya or the devil. So you want me ta tell ya 'bout the war?

CORNBREAD. Yeah, niggah. Tell me somethin' good.

BUGGY. Every time I done shot somebody I put his face ontopa theirs. Like mental Photoshop. Click, click. Eight-year-old boy wit' a AK — Tony C face. Sand niggah wit' a spooky eye — Tony C. face. Bitch covered head to toe wit' a blue scarf — Tony C. Somehow it made it easier. Make them into the evil you know. I don't know how many folk gone 'cause of me. I lost count. I done seen some thangs, Cornbread, but my mind somehow can rub out those memories like boot prints in the sand. It shift the shapes. But I can't never forget that day, maine. My mama was the baddest bitch on the block.

CORNBREAD. Sho'll in the hell was, maine ...

BUGGY. Beautiful to the point it look like she didn't belong here.

CORNBREAD. Belonged in a Jay-Z video. "Big Pimpin'/ spendin' cheese!"

BUGGY. "Spendin' cheese!" You know what I'm sayin'? She didn't pay nobody no nevermind and that why Tony C wanted her. He was a persistent fuck, but she kept turnin' him down 'til that one day. He just … took her. Broke down the door. I'm standin' there in my pajamas. "Go to school Buggy. Getcho lesson," she said, but I wouldn't leave her. They pushed her into that back room and locked the door. I sat in that den all mornin' and listened to my mama bein' took by a whole gang of niggahs.

CORNBREAD. Yeah … I 'member that, too.

BUGGY. At eight years old, I knew the world wun't right. Wun't gone ever be right. They left and Tony C said, "You a good boy." I went into her room, she layin' there, blood on her stomach and cum on her breath. "Close the door, Buggy, let Mama rest." She start hittin' that pipe hard after that. World wun't right ever since. Nobody ever kill theyself, Cornbread. 'Til this day, I say Tony C kilt my mama. *(Beat.)*

CORNBREAD. Let's do what we do then.

Scene 3

"Cornbread in the Oven"

Cornbread's unit. Crank is cutting Cornbread's hair with clippers.

CORNBREAD. I want you to line me up tight.

CRANK. Where Toyia at?

CORNBREAD. Gone.

CRANK. I sees that.

CORNBREAD. That's all you need to know.

CRANK. Hmmph.

CORNBREAD. Can you line my beard up a bit? *(Crank sighs and slides in front of him to line his beard. Cornbread looks deeps into her eyes. Crank smiles and continues cutting his hair.)* I love to see your smile.

CRANK. Well, sop it up 'cause it don't come too often.

CORNBREAD. Seem like you only do it when I'm around. *(Crank smiles even wider, emitting a laugh. Cornbread puts his ear to her belly. Beat.)* I don't hear nothin'.

CRANK. You ain't gone hear nothin' yet.

CORNBREAD. How long it take?

CRANK. Long enough to know that you won't be around.

CORNBREAD. You act like I'm movin' to China. I'm just movin' to Mississippi. It ain't nothin' but a forty-five-minute drive.

CRANK. Cornbread, I don't think it's yours.

CORNBREAD. Whatchoo mean? Who else you fuckin'?

CRANK. Who else *you* fuckin'?

CORNBREAD. Toyia.

CRANK. Exactly.

CORNBREAD. Awww, come on maine. You knew from the git go that was the bizness!

CRANK. I don't wantchoo.

CORNBREAD. You ain't ask me what I want.

CRANK. 'Cause you don't know what you want.

CORNBREAD. I know what I need.

CRANK. Hmmmph.

CORNBREAD. You. I need … you.

CRANK. Niggah, you is corny.

CORNBREAD. Wha?

CRANK. You want too much, Cornbread. From me and everybody else.

CORNBREAD. What the hell, wrong wit' that?

CRANK. It ain't good to want too much. End up disappointed at the end of thangs.

CORNBREAD. I promise. I ain't gone disappoint you. I wanna make you happy —

CRANK. You know she know.

CORNBREAD. She don't know nothin'.

CRANK. Yeah, she know.

CORNBREAD. How the fuck she know?

CRANK. I guess she called Cleo Psychic Friends, hell I don't know!

CORNBREAD. She don't know shit. She don't know nothin' 'bout this good lovin' right chere. *(He leans in to kiss Crank. She pushes him away.)* Oh, I ain't him. That what it is?

CRANK. No, you not. No matter how hard you try.

TOYIA. Ahem. *(Toyia is at the door. They both straighten up.)*

CORNBREAD. Do you believe in knockin'?

TOYIA. I didn't know I had to knock in my own muthafuckin' house. *(She carries in shopping bags.)*

CORNBREAD. Whatchoo done went done bought?

TOYIA. Stuff fo' our new house. I done got the layaway out from Target. *(Pronounced Tar-zhey. Beat.)*

CRANK. *(To Cornbread.)* That'll be fifteen. *(She holds out her hand.)*

CORNBREAD. Here. *(He gives her a crisp $50 bill. Toyia snatches it out of his hand.)*

TOYIA. Why you gone give this bitch a fifty? You ain't gave me nothin' but twenty-five dollars this morning.

CORNBREAD. Toyia, stay out my business. *(Crank quickly packs up her belongings.)*

CRANK. Keep it. Unlike you, I don't need na'an maine to take care of my ass.

TOYIA. Needin' and havin' are two entire different thangs, lil' mama.

CRANK. If it was left up to me, I wouldn't come over here.

TOYIA. Then don't, bitch. Ain't nobody done axed you to cut his head. You should be cuttin' it for free as much money he gives you for Cookie and that little cornbread muffin you got bakin' in the oven. *(Beat.)* What, y'all thank a bitch wun' gone find out about that, huh? Surprised he ain't make you go get that "fixed." *(Toyia has touched a nerve and Crank turns around eyes brimming red with fury.)*

CRANK. I don't use abortion like birth control, like *you*.

TOYIA. And I don't lose my babies over a little crack, like *you!* *(Cornbread steps in between the two.)*

CORNBREAD. I know y'all ain't fightin' over me.

TOYIA. You would like that fo' yo' lil' ego / wun't you?

CRANK. This ain't got nothin' to do witchoo!

TOYIA. Sho'll don't. But you should gone on and take it. Look like, you gone need all the help you can get … partnah. Word on the skreets, y'all ain't got nowhere to stay. I would let you chill up in my cut, but … we need a maid not a mistress. *(Toyia looks Cornbread up and down. Crank snatches the money out of Toyia's hands and walks out of the unit.)* I'll be over to get my tracks pult out.

Scene 4

"Big Mama's Plea (Case #AD1619)"

The Welfare Office. Big Mama has been standing in the wel-
fare line for the past three and a half hours. There are crying
children of all ages creating the kind of cacophony that causes
a mother's migraine.

A VOICE. Case number A.D. one six one nine.
BIG MAMA. Woohoo my dawgs was just a barkin'! You mind if
I take off my shoes? Thank ya darlin'. I been standin' in that hot
ass sun for what been like three hours. And y'all wonder why black
folk like to riot. Excuse me, ma'am. Where a needle and thread to
sew up my mouth? I'm one of them folks bein' moved out 'cause
the city done won the HOPE grant. Yes ... I live in Hurt Village,
ma'am. Yes, ma'am. Who you tellin'? I been livin' there over thirty
years and, yes, it has gone to hell in a handbasket, but it wun't
always like that. I 'member a time when folks kept they porch
clean, young men was respectful, didn't wear they shorts hangin' all
down they ass, there wun' a liquo' store on every corner and there
was grass ... Lawd there was grass. Seem like after Dr. King was
shot this neighborhood went down faster than a two-dollar hoe for
a ten-dollar bill, but I ain't here to give you a history lesson. Well,
I done got this here, uhm, paper in the mail sayin' I's been denied
Section 8 'cause I makes three hundred eighty-seven dollars ova
this here uhm, "public assistance maximum." Ma'am? I understand
that that's here the rules, but we all know the law can be changed
for folks who done done good, well ... I'm here 'cause we ain't got
nowhere else to go. They said we was gone be moved out to Raleigh
come this comin' Friday but 'cause I might have lied a little bit on
the application here, well, we might be out on the skreets, and I
gots a family to take care of — Oooooo! That nail polish look real
good on yo' toenails. What that is? Electric lightnin' blue? Look
real spiffy 'gainst yo' skin ma'am. You got some creamy skin —
Well, ma'am. Uhmm, I can't really go nowhere else. I gots my

grandbaby. Done come back from the war and he … sick. Yeah and his girlfriend there, and they gots a beautiful smart lil' girl — the best of both of them — and she gone be somethin'. Already bein' bussed out to Raleigh so, ma'am … ma'am … Ma'am LISTEN!!!! I don't mean to raise my voice, but ain't no other office to go to but this one. What, I'm trying to do a lil' betta for me and my family, and I gets punished for't? What that is? Y'all say y'all don't want a niggah on Welfare they get off it, they get them a lil' funky-ass job cleanin' up piss and shit and vomit and other unmentionables and you wanna drop 'em out the system faster than a hoe droppin' panties on the Auction Street corner. We just tryin' to get by. Three hundred eighty-seven dollars ain't nothin'. It ain't enough money to even put a down payment on a 'partment barely. It'll be gone takin' care of what I needs to take care of. I'll quit my job if I need to, but I need to be put back on the list. You see, ever since I was a lil' girl all I could dream about was the day I'd have my own room all to myself with a door that could close me off from the sorrow of my home. That's all I eva wanted ma'am was a lil' space of my own. I ain't like them other lazy niggahs. And I ain't raised no chillen up that way. We good clean livin' people, and, when we ain't, 'least we tryin' to be. Please, ma'am. *(She gets on her knees.)* Ma'am, I thank you for your kindness in advance if you do me this one favor. I don't ever wanna be out on them skreets like I been. Please … put me back where I belong.

Scene 5

"The Untouchables"

Night time. Cornbread's unit. The TV has on BET uncut. The latest soft-porn videos are spilling into the living room. Buggy, Cornbread, and Skillet are chillin' in the cut. Cornbread is counting money. Skillet is playing video games. Buggy is on the phone.

BUGGY. Whatchoo' talkin' 'bout? The ticket on that like fifty-five dollars apiece. It been ugly out here. It's clear though. Chopped up and clear. Call me back when you get on Auction. Bet. *(He hangs up the phone.)* That gone take us to our five hundred dollars today. We on fire, playas. *(Cornbread puffs on some weed.)*

SKILLET. So you like it?

CORNBREAD. Pussy-smellin' weed, dawg? This shit tight, but I don't know how it gone be I come home smellin' like weed *and* pussy. Toyia already snoopin' 'round and shit.

BUGGY. Yeah, we might have to put this on the backburner. But I likes yo' entrepreneurial spirit lil' bra. You gone be a good businessman.

CORNBREAD. "Pussy-smellin' weed." I like this lil' niggah righ' here. *(They give Skillet a pound and dap.)*

BUGGY. So this last shipment done turnt into the initial investment of Buggy Enterprises.

CORNBREAD. Buggy Enterprises?

BUGGY. Yeah, niggah. Cornbread Corner sound too-too —

SKILLET. Whack.

BUGGY. Hell, yeah.

CORNBREAD. No, it don't.

SKILLET. How 'bout Buggy, Cornbread 'n' Skillet Associates?

CORNBREAD. Hell, Cornbread 'n' Skillet sound better by itself.

SKILLET. Cornbread *in* a skillet.

CORNBREAD. Shut yo gay ass up. Ain't nobody puttin' they dick up in you.

BUGGY. What the hell you talkin' 'bout?

CORNBREAD. He comin' on to me and shit. Cornbread *in* a skillet.

BUGGY. That purple got you paranoid.

CORNBREAD. Do not!

BUGGY. Whatever, niggah. It need to be Buggy Enterprises 'cause I'm the boss of this operation.

CORNBREAD. How you gone come up and be the boss of this?

SKILLET. You been gone for I don't know how long.

BUGGY and CORNBREAD. Niggah, shut up!

CORNBREAD. Yeah, you have been gone for I don't know how long. I know the lay of the land betta than you. Follow a man who runnin' blind, we liable to catch a charge fo' real.

BUGGY. I'm a natural born killer.

SKILLET. I like that movie.

BUGGY and CORNBREAD. Niggah, SHUT up!

BUGGY. I'm tellin' you, niggah. I'm the smart one. That's how it always been. I'm the winner.

CORNBREAD. Oh, you the winner?

BUGGY. I win everything. From the baddest bitches to e'er fight. You said so yo'self. I'm a untouchable niggah.

CORNBREAD. How you untouchable?

BUGGY. 'CAUSE I AM!! AND DON'T LET NOBODY TELL YOU NO DIFFERENT! *(Buggy's hands begin to shake. Silence.)*

SKILLET. They say purple Kool-Aid get rid of the shakes. *(They look at him sharply.)*

CORNBREAD. I just wanna know why you thank you can come over here and put yo'self in a place you don't deserve to be. If anybody gone be the Kang of this op it should be me. Me. ME! *(Buggy catches another call. He takes it.)*

SKILLET. He do be gettin' mo' calls than you. And he just been here a minute. *(Cornbread stares at him.)* But on the other hand … nevermind. *(Buggy gets off the phone.)*

BUGGY. Take this to that crack house on Poplar and Keel. You know where that is?

CORNBREAD. Niggah, that's Tony C house. *(Beat.)*

BUGGY. I know. *(Skillet takes it. Looks at his leaders who are staring each other down. He opens the door and leaves.)*

Scene 6

"Synonyms"

Right after. Outside the unit. Cookie is examining her science experiment on her porch. Applying cocoa butter to his scars, Skillet looks down at her from Cornbread's porch. He gazes at her awhile.

SKILLET. I ... like ... yo' hair ... like ... that. *(Cookie ignores him. He cowers in slight embarrassment.)* It sho'll is hot out ... here.

COOKIE. It's Memphis. It's summer. DUH!

SKILLET. One of 'em jumped out.

COOKIE. Impossible.

SKILLET. Fo' real. I seen't it.

COOKIE. It's nine up in there. Niggah, you can't count.

SKILLET. I'm ugly, not dumb. *(Cookie counts.)*

COOKIE. Shit, one did get out. Fuckadoodle! My hypothesis gone be wrong.

SKILLET. No, it won't.

COOKIE. You don't even know what a hypothesis is! None of them supposeta get out. They ain't supposeta! Now, everybody gone laugh at me.

SKILLET. It ain't bad when everybody laugh at you. That mean you matter, even if it ain't by much.

COOKIE. How it get out? You musta came over here and knocked over my jar.

SKILLET. I ain't come nowhere near yo' ... porch. You ever thought 'bout the "exception to the rule," fool! Sometime shit go wrong for the right reason.

COOKIE. Exception to the rule, my black ass!

SKILLET. One of 'em just stuck wit' it a little longer than the rest, thass all. Didn't care 'bout bumpin' his bug head against the lid. 'Cause he kept on hittin' his feet on the jar bottom when he fell. And hell, one pain was easier to take than the other, so he kept on jumpin' 'cause he never stop believin' that one day that junt was

58

gone be blowed off. If not by God, then by his own goddamn self, so he formed a helmet of scars that covered his head so it wouldn't hurt no more. When them other mofos stopped jumpin', he jumped higher 'til finally he blowed the lid off. When he jumped out on the other side, he had a harder head and a bigger heart 'cause he didn't give up when every other niggah did. Exception ... to ... the rule ... Cookie.

COOKIE. That's the smartest thing you ever done said.

SKILLET. I 'member likin' science class — when I went. Like I said, I'm ugly, not dumb.

COOKIE. You ain't ugly either.

SKILLET. What, you got another ... synonym for me?

COOKIE. *(She smiles.)* Naw, I got an antonym for you.

SKILLET. Beautiful?

COOKIE. Naw ...

SKILLET. Pretty?

COOKIE. That for a girl.

SKILLET. Handsome?

COOKIE. That for a man. You ... cute.

SKILLET. *(Blushing.)* I'll take that. Well, Cookie ... you ... beautiful. *(He means it. Uncomfortable silence.)*

COOKIE. You lyin'.

SKILLET. Have you ever knowed me to lie?

COOKIE. You a niggah. You liable to lie to get some.

SKILLET. I don't wantcho goodies. I just ... I just ... thought ... that ... that I could give you a present before we go.

COOKIE. Where you movin' to?

SKILLET. Nowhere. Nowhere like the somewhere you goin'. *(He kisses her sloppily. She tenses, drowning in saliva. But then he kisses her softly. And softer still.)*

COOKIE. That's how kissin' feel?

SKILLET. Soft. Like that. *(Skillet being the socially inept being he is, gathers himself then runs away. Touching her lips, Cookie looks after him.)*

Scene 7

"Sand Niggahs"

Night. Cornbread's unit. Cornbread and Buggy have Nintendo guns in their hands. They are shooting at the TV screen playing Duck Hunt. *They are buzzed, dancing around with beer bottles in their hands.*

CORNBREAD.
 Get 'em high Get 'em loose off that fuckin' Grey Goose
 Get 'em high Get 'em loose tear the fuck up off this roof
 We gone burn it, crunk it up, tear da fuckin' club up
 Get 'em high, niggahs fly up to the sky
(Cornbread picks up the beat and Buggy flows with the chaotic frenzy of a man gone crazy.)
BUGGY.
 I'm a solja, thought I tolja nota boast but
 I'll stomp out any niggah who step too fuckin' close
 Stomp! Stomp! in da face wit' my combat boots
 I pop off e'er niggah, I don't care 'bout who I shoot
 I'm Scarface, niggah!
 Crates of cookies stacked high
 If you step up to me,niggah
 I'ma fly you to the sky
CORNBREAD and BUGGY.
 Get 'em high Get 'em loose off that fuckin' Grey Goose
 Get 'em high Get 'em loose tear the fuck up off this roof
 We gone burn it, crunk it up, tear da fuckin' club up
 Get 'em high, niggahs fly up to the sky
(They dance around.)
CORNBREAD. Maine, where the fuck Skillet at? We gone drank all this shit up fo' he get back. *(Buggy shoots at the screen.)*
BUGGY. Take that Tony C!
CORNBREAD. Two caps to the brain and then it'll all be over.
BUGGY. Thass all you man 'nough to pop off? Shit, I'll put fifty-

three bullets in that niggah dome. Rat-tat-tat-tat-tat-tat-tat. That's what we useta do. Anybody look at me funny they get it. *(Cornbread looks a little uneasy.)*

CORNBREAD. Yeah, right, niggah …

BUGGY. I ain't playin' witchoo. One straight to the dome. No problem. They pump yo' helmet full of that crunk music. It get 'side yo' head bring that terror into yo' dome. Get you crunked-up, fucked-up, tear da club up pumped. And pow. Pow. Pow. Shoot a muthafucka dead. You ain't never shot nobody?

CORNBREAD. Hell, naw, niggah. But I gotta gun though. Teach me.

BUGGY. What you wanna learn fo'? I'm the one that's gone do the do when it come down to it.

CORNBREAD. I might need to protect myself.

BUGGY. Niggah, it's on me.

CORNBREAD. Well, practice on me then.

BUGGY. Naw, naw, niggah. *(Cornbread mocks Tony C's walk.)*

CORNBREAD. I'm the Kang! I'm the Kang! *(Buggy demonstrates with the Nintendo gun.)*

BUGGY. Okay, first you get him in yo' sight line. Make sho' a vital organ come up clear in the circle window on the sight. Be quiet. Look at 'em. Look 'em in they eye if you can. Take a breath 'cause yo' finger gone be shakin'. Take another breath if yo' body shake. Then pull back and Pow! *(Cornbread pretends to fall dead on the floor.)* Pink mist all across yo' sight. See, I loved to kill them sand niggahs. They looked just like you.

CORNBREAD. Whatchoo talkin' 'bout? I'm black, niggah.

BUGGY. Hell, they the new niggahs of the earth. They useta look at me crazy. Could tell they was talkin' shit 'bout me. Could feel they voices crawl up under yo' skin. *(He mimics the sounds of the Arabic language.)* Just knew what the fuck they was sayin'. You see you get paranoid, Cornbread, of e'erbody and e'erthing. *(While Buggy speaks, he focuses his Nintendo gun on Cornbread. Cornbread laughs uneasily.)*

CORNBREAD. Niggah … you crazy.

BUGGY. Am I?

CORNBREAD. I ain't a fan of poppin' pills, but if you need to take a chill pill, I'm all for it. *(Buggy draws closer to Cornbread with his Nintendo gun on him.)*

BUGGY. Naw, I'm chillin' right here up in the cut. You know what else we would do to sand niggahs like you.

61

CORNBREAD. I don't know.

BUGGY. Take they daughters. Fuck 'em up the ass with a rifle. Maybe a broke beer bottle.

CORNBREAD. Niggah … thass disgusting.

BUGGY. *(Laughing at it all.)* Oh, what you don't like to hear my freaky tales. You still like pussy, don'tcha?

CORNBREAD. I don't like cut-up pussy —

BUGGY. Y'all all look the same. Couldn't tell if y'all was naughty or nice. Shit, 'least they got uniforms over here. If you a Crip or G.D., you shoot the niggah wearin' red. If you a Blood, you shoot the niggah wearin' blue. Niggahs is real simple. They make they self easy targets. But over there, they just wearin' whatever. *(Buggy draws closer to Cornbread's head.)*

CORNBREAD. I ain't nothin' like 'em … *(Buggy puts the Nintendo gun to Cornbread's head. Beat.)*

BUGGY. You are. Can I trust you, sand niggah? *(Beat.)*

CORNBREAD. Yeah, yeah … partnah. We gone take down his set together. *(Buggy withdraws his gun. Beat.)* What they done done to you?

BUGGY. "They" didn't do nothin.' I been trainin' for this my whole life. *(Buggy returns back to his game of playing Duck Hunt. Cornbread stares at him. Buggy is oblivious.)*

Scene 8

"The Bank of America"

Later still that night. Buggy walks into the unit. Big Mama is getting ready for work. The Cosby Show or a similar late-night syndicated sitcom is on the TV in the background.*

BUGGY. You still here?

BIG MAMA. Gettin' ready to go to work.

BUGGY. Constantly on that night-shift grind.

---

* See Special Note on Songs and Recordings on copyright page.

BIG MAMA. I'm 'bout to go work a double.

BUGGY. Here. *(He hands her a roll of money.)*

BIG MAMA. *(Hesitantly.)* That fast, huh?

BUGGY. Always one of the slickest hustlers in Memphis. That should tide you over for a bit. *(She looks at the money balanced in her palm.)*

BIG MAMA. Thank you. *(Big Mama puts it in her bra and starts shuffling out the door. Buggy sits on the couch to relax his feet.)*

BUGGY. I told you I'd take care of you didn't I? The boy is back. The good old boy is back to take over that "Million Dollar Track." *(Big Mama stops. She turns around.)*

BIG MAMA. This ain't for long, Buggy, just 'til we get back on our feet.

BUGGY. I know, Big Mama —

BIG MAMA. We ain't gotta do this forever.

BUGGY. Don't worry, I'll do it 'til forever if I got to —

BIG MAMA. You like doin' this?

BUGGY. I like survivin'.

BIG MAMA. Seem like you like doin' this.

BUGGY. I like survivin'. Don't you? *(Beat.)*

BIG MAMA. Buggy, I got down on my knees today for the first time in I don't know how long.

BUGGY. You prayed?

BIG MAMA. Naw, I begged. But to me, seem like ain't no difference 'tween the two. Every time I done got on my knees I never hear what I wanna hear. Never get what I need to get. Guess it 'cause God only take care of fools and babies, the rest of us gotta get along by our damn selves.

BUGGY. I must be a fool then —

BIG MAMA. Naw, you my baby, Buggy. The only thang I got left. The only thang I got left from her ... We done had some hard times you and me. Me and you both runnin' in and out of crackhouses.

BUGGY. Big Mama —

BIG MAMA. Constantly bailin' her out of jail —

BUGGY. I don't wanna hear this right now —

BIG MAMA. Findin' her on her knees in alleys. Yankin' her out the back of cars —

BUGGY. Big Mama, PLEASE!!

BIG MAMA. My knees got rubbed raw from dealin' wit' that girl. You'd thank I was a fuckin' prostitute the way my knees got to lookin'. I musta did something wrong in another life, 'cause the more I talked to the sky, the more the moon laughed at me. When I was walkin' back home, all I could see was Tiffany … Tiffany. All these lil' Tiffany's wobbling they way down that "Million Dollar Track" trying to make they way to the sky. I don't know what gone happen now. I'm a fool to even dream it'll be different, but I can't take this no mo', Buggy … I just … can't … *(She takes the money and gingerly places it in his hand.)*

BUGGY. Take the money, Big Mama.

BIG MAMA. That money got blood on it.

BUGGY. TAKE the money, Big Mama.

BIG MAMA. People tears on it.

BUGGY. Big Mama, what I say—

BIG MAMA. It gone kill you.

BUGGY. No, it ain't —

BIG MAMA. It kilt yo' mama. *(Breath.)* You used to be such a good boy.

BUGGY. Don't start.

BIG MAMA. Such a good, *good* boy —

BUGGY. I AM NOT A GOOD BOY. QUIT CALLIN' ME THAT! Good don't live here in the projects. Look out the window. Just a bunch of niggahs and bitches runnin' amuck havin' babies they don't need.

BIG MAMA. You thank you betta than them? You ain't no betta than them.

BUGGY. You right. I ain't. Thass the problem. This shit can't be stopped.

BIG MAMA. Buggy, things can be stopped. Now. You might can't save yo' daughter, but you can save yo' grandbaby, you my baby —

BUGGY. You can't save me. Nobody can save me.

BIG MAMA. Yes, I can, if you just let me —

BUGGY. Oh, I see what it is. My glove supplier gettin' all guilty on me. You guilty? You feel bad about my mama? Well, you should. Crack ain't kill her. *You* kilt her. Every time you smacked, cussed her, downed her, you kilt her. Everybody beatin' on her from Tony C to you to the whole entire hood — *(Big Mama smacks Buggy.)*

BIG MAMA. Yo' soul so curdled up inside done got to lookin' like buttermilk left out in the sun too long. *(Beat.)* I wun't the best mama in the world, but who the fuck is? I'm here, Buggy. I'm here. You done gotcho ass a second chance at life, most niggahs don't get one. Take it. Take the right way, not the left way 'cause you thank that's the only one you got left.

BUGGY. Take the money, Big Mama.

BIG MAMA. No.

BUGGY. Take it!

BIG MAMA. I'm goin' to work. I'm gone works for mine.

BUGGY. You think you can bring in five hundred a day? Two G's a week? You ain't nothin' but a janitor. *(Big Mama heads for the screen door.)* Big Mama, you take this money, now. I been workin' all damn day to get this.

BIG MAMA. I said I don't want it.

BUGGY. Cookie need that poster board … *(Beat. Big Mama turns away.)* So you done woke up and smelt the coffee, huh?

BIG MAMA. Yeah, bitches always do it faster than the niggahs. *(Big Mama walks out the door.)*

Scene 9

"The Insurrection"

Later that same night. Cornbread and Buggy are under the Auction Street sign.

CORNBREAD. Where the fuck is that maine? He been gone all night. That niggah went and smoked all that shit up. Bet!

BUGGY. He prolly just got held up with somethin'.

CORNBREAD. For three hours?

BUGGY. Hell, I don't know!

CORNBREAD. Maybe he fuckin' some bitch. *(Beat.)*

BUGGY and CORNBREAD. Nanh! *(They laugh. Beat.)*

BUGGY. Big Mama ain't take the money.

CORNBREAD. Hell, then give it to me.

BUGGY. Naw, she just on that savior tip. But when she ain't got nowhere to go, then I'll be her muthafuckin' savior. *(Ebony walks in. He is shaking. Tony C is walking up behind him.)*

CORNBREAD. What the hell wrong wit' that niggah? *(Ebony leans against a pole. Beat. He vomits.)* Drunk ass.

BUGGY. Naw … he ain't drunk …

TONY C. Niggah, didn't I tell you! Aim at the side of his head. Don't listen to nothin' nobody tell y'all. Bitch-ass, niggah. Got that niggah blood all on my K-Swiss. Now, I'ma have to buy a new pair. *(Ebony vomits again.)* Awwwww, just who I been lookin' for. Ran into y'all lil' boy. Down there on Poplar and Keel. *(Cornbread looks at Buggy.)* It's funny, when that niggah got a gun in his face, he sho'll do speak fast. Speak so fast he start stutterin' and shit. "T-tt-tton-n-ny C-c-c." I heard 'em loud and clear though.

CORNBREAD. Tony. C., maine, we 'um —

BUGGY. Where Skillet?

TONY C. Unh, unh, unh … I ask the questions round here. What, y'all thank a niggah wun't gone find out? Buggy and Cornbread — what he say, Ebony?

EBONY. Associates.

CORNBREAD. It's Enterprises.

TONY C. Awwww, my bad, niggah. Excuse me. That was a stupid move, Buggy. I ain't knownt you to be stupid. Cornbread? Maybe. But *you?* You gone just up and ignore my proposition and hook up wit' this here twinkie-colored niggah, this South Memphis sellin' niggah on my muthafuckin' turf, niggah — *(Ebony dry heaves again.)*

BUGGY. Where Skillet at?

EBONY. *(Weeping.)* Gone.

TONY C. Niggah, if you don't be quiet, you gone end up where yo' friend is. We had to take him to the other side of the river, if you know what I'm sayin'. I don't take kindly to folk thankin' they can run me. I ain't no bitch. I can't be runt.

CORNBREAD. Tony C, maine, you know we was just —

TONY C. Fuckin' around, yeah, I know. Y'all gone have to come up off all that prof'. Can't be sellin' shit to my customers on my turf tryin' to run me out. Y'all worser than these white muthafuckas. Thankin' they can come run me out of business. Can take over my muthafuckin' real estate. *(He screams to no one in particular.)* THIS IS PRIME MUTHAFUCKIN' REAL ESTATE. I'm the KANG. I can't be runt.

CORNBREAD. How 'bout we give you twanky-five percent?

TONY C. Niggah, is you crazy?

CORNBREAD. But, that's our money, niggah.

TONY C. My territory, *my* money, niggah.

CORNBREAD. That ain't fair.

TONY C. That's the politickin' of the projects. I RUN THIS BITCH!!! Now give me that muthafuckin' prof'.

BUGGY. Take it.

CORNBREAD. *(Whispering to Buggy.)* Niggah, is you crazy?

BUGGY. He can have it, only one thang. *(To Tony C.)* You gone have to take it from me, if you want it.

TONY C. I'm all about takin', niggah, ye'en know?

CORNBREAD. Maine, we don't want no problems. *(Cornbread reaches in his waistband for a gun.)*

TONY C. *(To Cornbread.)* Touché ... niggah. You thank you fast enough.

BUGGY. *I* am.

TONY C. Oh, solja boy, quit it.

BUGGY. Ain't no hoe up in me.

TONY C. Yes, there is. Yo' mama. *(Beat. Buggy charges toward Tony C and in one swoop lifts him off the ground with his bare hands. They struggle intensely.)* You wanna kill me! Kill me! I double-dog dare you. KILL ME, NIGGAH!

CORNBREAD. Buggy, you ain't got the gun!

TONY C. Kill me! Please, kill me!

BUGGY. I don't need no fuckin' gun.

TONY C. *(Hoarse.)* Kill me, niggah ...

BUGGY. You want me to kill you?

TONY C. Please ... kill ... me ...

BUGGY. You'd love that wouldn't you? The Kang can't stand to see his kingdom go.

TONY C. Kill me, niggah ... Kill ... me *(Buggy has Tony C up in the air with his bare hands. Tony C's feet dangle trying to touch the crumbling ground. Buggy stares into Tony C's eyes that are rolling into the back of his head. His huge hands are squeezing the life out of him. Police sirens can be heard.)*

CORNBREAD. Niggah, leave his monkey ass alone! Somebody done called the po-po!

BUGGY. Naw, niggah. I'ma grant him his wish. *(Buggy squeezes harder. Tony C chokes fighting to inhale. Beat. Buggy lets him go. Tony C falls down to the ground.)*

TONY C. *(Coughing.)* You thank I like doin' this shit? I got to! Thass all we know. This all we know ...

BUGGY. Naw, niggah. Thass all *you* know.

CORNBREAD. Break out, niggah, now! Come on! COME ON! *(Cornbread runs off. Buggy stares at Ebony. Beat. He runs after Cornbread. Tony C looks around and begins to gather himself together.)* TONY C. *(Hoarse.)* Ebony, hand me my shoe. Ebony, hand me my muthafuckin' K-Swiss.

EBONY. Kill yo'self fool, ole' Elvis Presley – lookin-ass niggah. *(Ebony busts out running as the police sirens engulf the night.)*

Scene 10

"Ace Boon Coons"

Night. The unit. Gunshots pop off. Crank is folding up clothes. There are police lights and sirens coming from the outside.

CRANK. What the fuck is goin' on? *(Bang. Bang. Bang on the unit door.)* Who the fuck bangin' on my / muthafuckn' do' like they crazy?

TOYIA. It's me, bitch! Open up! It's me! *(Crank undoes the three locks to open the door. Toyia enters in a panic.)* This day is just fucked-up from the rooda to da tooda. First off. Girl, folk say they done fount Skillet wit' a bullet in his head on the playground. And po-po got Cornbread down at the jail house on some trumped-up dope charge. Cornbread call me say some deal wit' Tony went awry like a muthafucka.

CRANK. What!

TOYIA. Girl, I'ma need some money for bail. He done fo' shore-ly! One hundred fifty thousand dollars. I need a fifteen-thousand-dollar bail bond. Thass all our scrilla! Say he had that pure*dee* white on him. I mean what the fuck! Them cops call theyself investigatin' some shit all up in the cut. God know what they gone find, you'd think Cornbread be smarter than that. Hell, he half white!

CRANK. Just calm down, Toyia!

TOYIA. *(Weeping.)* I don't know what to do. What the fuck am I gone do? Cornbread … what about my Cornbread? *(She falls down to the ground.)*

CRANK. Bitch, pull yo'self together! *(Beat.)*

TOYIA. You my girl right? You my ace boon coon right?

CRANK. Yeah, bitch.

TOYIA. You'd be down for me like I been down for you, righ?

CRANK. Yeah, yeah, yeah.

TOYIA. Well, I need you to hold somethin' for me.

CRANK. Like some money?

TOYIA. Naw. *(She passes a baby bag to Crank.)*

CRANK. Hell, naw. I ain't keepin' LaQwanna all night!

TOYIA. Bitch, quit actin' a damn fool! *(Crank looks in.)*

CRANK. Product.

TOYIA. Cornbread say Tony C after him fo' sho. Tony C gone come for this product ... or me ... I gotta get gone ... Come on, Crank. That niggah kill babies and shit.

CRANK. No, I can't be by that.

TOYIA. He bury folks alive and shit!

CRANK. I can't be by that!

TOYIA. He rape bitches with brooms and shit!

CRANK. I said NO!

TOYIA. Come on, you my BITCH! What happen that time I kicked Mr. Stokley in the mouth for hemmin' you up in the P.E. closet? What 'bout that time, Crank? You owe me, girl.

CRANK. I can't be by that stuff.

TOYIA. Well, if you can't do it for me, then do it for him. Cornbread done took care of you and yours. You owe him. If you don't owe me, at least you owe him. Besides, you been off, like, three years, bitch. And plus you ... ya know ... you —

CRANK. Pregnant.

TOYIA. Yeah bitch, I know. I know ... Look I wouldn't put you in a situation you could'n handle. That shit ain't got no hold on you. But if they find this shit on me, in that house ... come on. We'd do it for you.

CRANK. What if they come up in here and start sniffin' round here?

TOYIA. We'd do it for you. Hell, we ace boon coons, ya know what I'm sayin'? Just hold it 'til this all ova wit. *(Beat.)*

CRANK. You gone get it first thang?

TOYIA. First thang in the mornin'. *(Toyia gives her a pound and a snap.)* We ace boon coons fo' life, bitch.

Scene 11

"The Lynching"

*In the blue flicker of the TV, Crank stares at the diaper bag.
Looks away. She tries desperately to occupy herself. Then she
opens it.*

TV ANCHOR VOICE. Breaking from Action News Five —
Memphis police units found the body of a young African-American
male, age fifteen to eighteen, on Auction in the infamous Hurt
Village projects in North Memphis. Police say the youth was most
likely the victim of a gang initiation. Police charged an unidentified
African-American male who was caught fleeing the crime site with
a concealed weapon — *(Crank turns off the TV. She takes the antennae off the set. She then takes a crack cookie from the stash. She goes to
the kitchen to get a spoon. Finds a lighter. Lights up. She takes antennae and sucks in the smoke rising from the spoon. As she smokes, she rises
high in the air as if she's levitating.)*
CRANK.
    Dear Cookie, I hope you find this letter
    You won't be able to because I can't write it
    I can only spin the memories
    Unwind the facts in my mind
    As this rock makes my thoughts implode
    Onto one another and hide behind
    Prison walls of project cement
    Stone the house we call home
    If you only knew I thought in poetic slants, diatribes
    That my mind held more words
    Than the largest dictionary could ever find
    That often I cannot heave my brain into my mouth
    To impress redress the mask I die behind.
    These are the thoughts of a druggie's
    coked-out-choked-out wired mind
    I can't seem to crack the safe I've hid my heart in

As I think about how I've never hugged you Cookie
My Cookie monster. I don't know how to begin
How to open my arms wide
Stretch my neck to a caving sky
Say those words my dictionary hearts
But my mouth fail to
"I love you."
Never heard those words said
Said them to niggahs as they fucked my brains out
Only to find the more you say it the less it means
Like sayin' niggah, bitch, or please
I need you to think that I'm a queen
Don't abide these diatribes
Just the thoughts of a dying druggie's mind.
My finger aches to wrap around your wrist
In a last moment mother-daughter tryst
I hope this body'll you'll never find
I wish you can capture my words as I think them into the sky.
I'll see you again beautiful girl as I vomit out
These last thoughts of a druggie's
Coked-out-choked-out wired mind.
(She has smoked the entire rock. Gone.)

Scene 12

"The Pledge of Allegiance"

Next day. Inside the unit. Buggy is hurriedly packing his things. Crank enters with eyes rimming red. She drags Cookie who has a jacket tied around her waist.

CRANK. And get in that house!
COOKIE. I don't wanna go, there no mo'! Fuck school!
CRANK. Buggy, give me yo belt.
BUGGY. What she done did?
CRANK. Actin' too grown for her damn good.

COOKIE. I don't wanna do it!

CRANK. It don't matter what you don't wanna do, you do what that teacher say. You mind them. You stand when that teacher tell you to stand, nah. I ain't gone tell you no mo'.

COOKIE. I hate you!

CRANK. She sho'll is doin' a lotta hatin' lately. I need to send you back to Humes. Gettin' too opinionated. Don't worry. I'ma beat the opinions right out of ya. You say the muthafuckin' pledge of allegiance.

BUGGY. What?

CRANK. That teacher tellin' her to stand up and lead the class in the pledge of allegiance and this lil' heifer gone say, "Naw!"

COOKIE. Idn' want to.

CRANK. Tell him what you said. Tell it Cookie!

COOKIE. I ain't gone pledge allegiance to a flag that don't pledge allegiance to me. *(Silence.)* Freedom of speech —

CRANK. Shut up, in the projects ain't no freedom of speech. You gone get it. I'm tired of all this goddamn back talk. You already know my nerves is bad. Get in that room. You gone strip down.

BUGGY. You ain't got to do all that …

CRANK. Naw, it's about time she learned her lesson. *(Cookie begins to sob uncontrollably.)*

BUGGY. Crank, she ain't did nothin' that bad.

CRANK. She need to go to school and get her lesson. She don't need to be kicked out, 'cause she gone be somebody, now strip the fuck down. Take it off! Everything! And get in that room!

BUGGY. Alright, Crank, you gettin' a lil' too crunk.

CRANK. Niggah, I ain't got crunk yet! And shut up, 'fo' I beat yo' ass, too. *(Crank goes into one of the boxes and she pulls out an extension cord.)* Strip! *(She goes over to Cookie and starts pulling at her clothes.)*

BUGGY. Crank, you want me to beat yo' ass?

CRANK. I'ma raise my chile the way I wanna, you gone come over here and stop me? You can't stop shit. As far as I'm concerned you ain't my babydaddy. You gone come up in here you been gone for God know how long and you thank you can say shit about my chile.

BUGGY. She mine, too.

CRANK. You sholl didn't act like it. Where you been? Where the letters from over there you said you was gone send us?

BUGGY. If I sent them you couldn't read 'em no how.

CRANK. Yo mammy, niggah. *(She continues to strip Cookie naked.)*

BUGGY. Fuck you, you snagatooth bitch.

CRANK. You ain't nothin' but a coward. You been a coward yo' whole life. You scared of Tony, you scared of this and that. You a pill-poppin' triflin' son of a — *(She looks at the back of Cookie's school uniform. There is a deep crimson red blood stain on her bottom. She's sobbing so badly that she's hiccupping.)*

COOKIE. I didn't wanna stand ... I didn' wanna stand. *(Silence.)*

BUGGY. Look what you done did.

CRANK. Well, she just shoulda tolt somebody. *(Beat.)*

BUGGY. Go put you some clean clothes on. Gone to the back, nah. Gone. *(Cookie slowly gathers the clothes her mother ripped from her body and walks to the back room.)*

CRANK. So she just shoulda tolt somebody then I wouldn' have to whup her. *(Crank stands there shaking, twitching.)*

BUGGY. You back on that white, ain't ya? *(Silence.)* You should be 'shamed of yo'self.

CRANK. How come? You 'shamed of yo'self? You sellin' it. Sellin' it to e'erbody. This shit got me on lock, maine. Ain't no runnin' from this shit. You walked out damn near ten years ago and now you wanna be here? For what? For what, WHAT? Dangle a piece of candy in front of our heart? Make it break a lil' more. When Cookie was growin' up she would walk round here askin' me, who her daddy was, where her daddy was. I almost wanted to tell her that I didn't know who her daddy was. I was willin' to label myself a hoe 'cause I couldn't get her daddy to love me enough to stick around to love her enough.

BUGGY. I ain't have enough money back then —

CRANK. Fuck the money, Buggy. "Why my daddy don't love me, Ma? Why my daddy don't send me birthday cards, Mama? Why I got his last name but I ain't neva seen his face?" Yeah, Buggy. Money don't answer them questions no matter how hard you try. I got to be makin' shit up. Did you see how proud she was of you? I'm sure you bein' a soldier satisfied e'er fantasy in her head. "That's why my daddy couldn't be there for me. That why, he was protectin' me from terrodom" — or terrorists or whatever the fuck you niggahs wanna call it. Her daddy was a fighter. Didn't know her daddy was a fuckin' doughboy not no hero! Her heart's the spittin' image of yourn, but you don't see it, do you?

BUGGY. Yes, I do.

CRANK. Well, be the daddy yo' daddy couldn' be for you, my daddy couldn' be for me, e'er niggah daddy couldn' be for them.

BUGGY. I can't be her daddy. I'm all messed up inside, Crank.
CRANK. Maine, who you tellin'? She gone be messed up if she neva know the other half of her. Sometimes I look at her and I hate myself. Yeah, I just can't believe I done brought another lil' black girl into this worl'. This worl' ain't built fo' beautiful brown black girls. The worl' ignore her, kick her when it's suppose to love her, bite her, when it's suppose to kiss her, tell her she ugly when she really pretty, rape her and blame it on her, piss on her stomach, cum on her face and say that the way to make a dollar, shake what ya mama gave you, not knowin' that what her mama gave her can't be bought. That her pussy is priceless. A lil' black girl got a hard load to carry. Sometimes I look at her and wish she ain't never been born. Not because I don't love her but because I love her with all my heart. Now is you gone be the worl' or her daddy? 'Cause I tell ya one thing, all her mama is is a lil' black girl who believed what the world done tol' her. Please take her from me.
BUGGY. I can't. I can't. I gotta get gone, Crank. I gotta —
CRANK. Yeah, I know. I just thought. I'd ask. *(Beat.)*
BUGGY. Why'd you do it? Why'd you go back on it?
CRANK. *(Shrugging her shoulders.)* That's the one thing that'll do a niggah in. Boredom and chaos, Buggy. Boredom and chaos.

Scene 13

"The Door of No Return"

Outside the unit. Buggy goes outside. Cookie is on the electricity box, consoling herself. Buggy walks down to the box.

BUGGY. You mind I kick it witchu for a hot minute?
COOKIE. Suit yo'self. I'm tryin' to kill myself. They say if you sit on the box for two hours it blow up. Straight into the sky. Like fireworks. I'll split in half. Like yo' friend.
BUGGY. But you ain't gone wanna do that 'cause nobody'll wanna look at you durin' yo' funeral. *(Cookie spits onto the ground.)* That ain't befittin' a young lady.

74

COOKIE. Oh, so now you wanna teach me how to be a lady?

BUGGY. Actually, yes. I wanna tell you 'bout the birds and the bees. I mean, since you a woman now.

COOKIE. Don't worry. I know all about it. A boy put his wee-wee in a girl mouth. She swallow his seeds and it go down into her belly and then nine months later she blowed up bigger than a house. That's why I won't let a boy nowhere near these lips. Peaches be lettin' boys skeet up in her mouth. I ain't 'bout to get preggers. Nozzir not me.

BUGGY. What you call it?

COOKIE. Preggers —

BUGGY. That ain't the way it happen. He don't put cum inside her mouth to get her ... preggers —

COOKIE. Yes, he do —

BUGGY. No, it's her legs.

COOKIE. How it gone go inside her leg?

BUGGY. Not inside, I mean *between* her legs.

COOKIE. Like where the pee come out?

BUGGY. Naw. See ... there's another hole. Below the pee-pee hole.

COOKIE. I got two holes down there?

BUGGY. In the front ... yeah ... .

COOKIE. Hmmph. That's interesting.

BUGGY. That's the way it is. The birds and the bees.

COOKIE. For real?

BUGGY. Mmmmphmm.

COOKIE. For real! Then how come Peaches preggers then if she only let them skeet up in her mouth?

BUGGY. Peaches prolly ain't tellin' the truth of thangs.

COOKIE. Yeah, she is. She my bestus friend.

BUGGY. "Best" friend.

COOKIE. Oh, my bad. "*Best* friend." She tell me everything. Well, maybe not as much as she use to. I barely see her since I started getting bussed over there.

BUGGY. To the white kids?

COOKIE. I'm the only one there.

BUGGY. I know how that feel.

COOKIE. You was the only niggah up in yo' platoon?

BUGGY. Yeap, bunch of cracker boys from Kentucky, Arkansas, and a whole slew from Peoria, Illinois, for some reason.

COOKIE. I'ma go them places when I become a flight attendant.

BUGGY. Well you gone have to learn how to talk right. 'Cause if you can talk right you can go anywhere you wanna. Be anything you wanna. Leave anytime you wanna.

COOKIE. Like you, huh?

BUGGY. Like me. Yeah, you can go to the Philippines, Germany, hell, Africa if you wanna.

COOKIE. You ain't comin' back, is ya? *(Beat.)*

BUGGY. No. *(Cookie accepts his answer, then smiles to herself.)*

COOKIE. I'd be scared to go there.

BUGGY. Where?

COOKIE. To Africa.

BUGGY. How come? I lived there for a hot minute.

COOKIE. A real hot minute, I bet.

BUGGY. *(To himself.)* That's where it all started.

COOKIE. You wun't rollin' round in the bushes with some cheetahs and apes, was you?

BUGGY. Well, ain't no cheetahs up in Ghana and that's where I was. I was fully expectin' niggahs to have bones in they noses and shit, but naw. They look just like me. I blended right in, boy. Right in. I met one of them bougie-ass niggahs went on vacation there. Say they went to some museum called the "Door of No Return." I decide I'ma go. I go through this tour company, and they take us into this cave. Tour man say that they would have two thousand niggahs in a stone room no bigger than two of these mufuckin' units. Two thousand packed. You run yo' hands along the wall and there are these big-ass dents. Waist high. The tour man say that's how much shit had collected. Imagine two thousand muthafuckas walkin' 'round waist high in shit. Look up about two stories and there was three windows lettin' air come up in the cut. Butcha can't git away from dat smell, maine.

COOKIE. 'Least they had windows.

BUGGY. Yeah, but they was so far away. See, the windows was for the ocean water. Now, if the ocean git high enough, water would splash in and rinse the shit away. Imagine mufuckas hopin' and prayin' water would somehow stream in to wash they hell away. Maybe even hopin' to drown. But then the tour man took us to a place for them unruly niggahs. The sun from the windows was sheddin' light on this hallway leadin' to a small openin'. It was a hole that come up to my waist. One foot in, you vanished into darkness. Nothin'. Black. Pitch black. I placed my hand inside that hole and that when I felt somethin'. Like smooth scoops in stone. I asked "What this?" The tour man say, "The slave scratches." With my hand, I read them bumps and valleys scratched into those walls by fingers trying to break through stone. He said e'ey slave that went into that hole died there. That's where it all started. Been trying to claw our way out ever since.

COOKIE. Seem like if e'ery niggah went over there and felt that wall, they'd live dey life a lil' different. *(But Buggy is not listening. He is staring at the graffiti tag. He reads it.)*

BUGGY. *"Das Haus des jammers."*

COOKIE. That's the Hurt Village code. When we tag other projects that's the letters we write. They say aliens came from out the sky and put them words outside the complex gate. Never knownt what it mean though.

BUGGY. It's German. It mean "The house of sorrow."

Epilogue

"The Demolition"

Outside the units. Cookie stands beneath the Auction Street sign. She is playing with her beloved dollhouse on the ground. The "Hurt Village is falling down" refrain is heard softly beneath.

COOKIE. They ain't pick up Skillet body 'til the next day. Some of the kids was playin' outside that mornin' so we got to walk right up to the body. See it. They ain't even cover him up. Just left him like that. Policeman say, "Let 'em see it. Teach these lil' niggahs a lesson." He was black. Po-po only come for the dead. They don't come for the livin'. They don't care about them folk. Just the dead. And they barely care 'bout them. Ashes to ashes, dust to dust. These project walls will crumble to the ground, and the tears and bloodshed will soon be forgotten. Big Mama got us back on the HOPE list, under one condition — my mama can't live wit' us since she got back on that shit. So we movin' on to Raleigh. Big

Mama my mama now. Daddy — I mean, Buggy. He gone again. I try to act like he was never here. Like them two weeks was a dream or somethin'. Like it never happened. Some say it take a village to raise a chile. Some time the child gotsta raise they goddamn self. I believes that. But no matter how the Hurt was, I'ma be a Hurt Village Hustler, for life, for LIFE! Whaaaa! WHAAAAA! I ain't sad and all, but uhm … I'ma miss shit. *(As she says the other characters' names, a light comes up on them standing in various places on the outside of the project building, as if they are dolls in the dollhouse of her imagination.)* Ebony checkin' niggahs on the corner. Toyia givin' her coochie lessons. Cornbread, my real daddy. How Skillet called me beautiful. Hell, even Tony C. *(The lights slowly fade on them.)* They all gone. I wonder how they gone be, but 'til we meet again, if we ever meet again. I got 'em in my rhyme and in my heart and in my mind. *(She begins a beat on the Auction Street sign pole. It rings with a metallic clang, underscoring her chant.)*

This be the war/ungh/this be the war/ungh
This be the war/ungh/this be the war/ungh, ungh
This be the war/ungh/this be the war
This be the war/ungh/this be the war/ungh
This be the war/ungh/this be the war/ungh, ungh
The is be the war/ungh/this be the war

(The engine sound of construction trucks can be heard rising over the refrain until it drowns Cookie out and all we see is her jookin', floating, flying beneath a fading lamp light under the Auction Street sign.)

End of Play

PROPERTY LIST

Army-green electric utility box
Cardboard boxes for moving
Comb
Beer
Woman's shoe
Refrigerator
JC Penney catalog
Publishers Clearing House mailer
Pocketbook
Dollhouse and dolls
Kool cigarettes and lighter or matches
Money; roll of money
Styrofoam plate
Popcorn
Makeshift grill
Metal barrel, pole, empty glass bottles used as ad-hoc instruments
Package of drugs
Cosmetology gear stored in plastic containers
Backpack
Mason jar with fleas
Glass of water
Water pitcher or bottle
Duffel bag
Red platform heels
Orthopedic shoes
Bottles of pills
English homework
Bottle
Letter
Blunt (for smoking)
2 pair surgical gloves
Baking soda, pot of boiling water and lighter (for making crack)
Hair clippers
Target shopping bags
Phone
Nintendo video game, guns and console; Duck Hunt game
Marijuana
Cocoa butter

Clothes for folding
Door locks
Diaper bag
Crack cookie
Spoon
TV antennae
Extension cord

SOUND EFFECTS

Chorus of children singing
TV
Crunk music and crunk drone
Bottle being thrown
Yelling
Knocking on screen door
Gunshots
Car pulling up and passing cars
Car horn
Car door slam .
Police sirens
Banging on door
Metallic clang
Construction trucks